Sovereign Grace Against the Gangrene of Arminianism
by Richard Resbury
with chapters by C. Matthew McMahon

Copyright Information

Sovereign Grace Against the Gangrene of Arminianism
by Richard Resbury, with chapters by C. Matthew McMahon
Edited by Therese B. McMahon

Copyright © 2025 by Puritan Publications and A Puritan's Mind

Some language and grammar has been updated from the original manuscript. Any change in wording or punctuation has not changed the intent or meaning of the original author(s), and has been made to aid the modern reader.

Published by Puritan Publications
A Ministry of A Puritan's Mind
Crossville, TN
www.apuritansmind.com
www.puritanpublications.com
www.gracechapeltn.com

All rights reserved. No part of this publication may be reproduced, stored in a retrieval system or transmitted in any form by any means, electronic, mechanical, photocopy, recording or otherwise, without the prior permission of the publisher, except as provided by USA copyright law.

This paperback first edition, 2025
Electronic edition, 2025
Manufactured in the United States of America

ISBN: 978-1-62663-509-8
eISBN: 978-1-62663-508-1

Table of Contents

Meet Richard Resbury 4

Richard Resbury Against Arminianism 8

To the Reader 15

The First Sermon 19

The Second Sermon 35

The Third Sermon 57

The Fourth Sermon 74

The Fifth Sermon 84

The Sixth Sermon: 98

Other Works Published by Puritan Publications that Deal with the Gangrene of Arminianism 115

Meet Richard Resbury
By C. Matthew McMahon, Ph.D., Th.D.

Richard Resbury (1607-1674), sometimes recorded as *Resburie* or *Rasbury*, was born in 1607 in the quiet hamlet of Kirkby Underwood, Lincolnshire, England. His baptism on September 7, 1606, preceded his remarkable life, and from his earliest days, his roots were set deep in the soil of a devout and large English family. He was one of eleven children born to Isaac Resburie and Alice Resburie, whose sprawling household must have buzzed with energy and the cadence of theological discussions in a time of great religious turbulence.

Richard's siblings—William, Adryan, John, Elizabeth, Anne, Alice, Adryan (the younger), Mary, Kateren, and Frauncis—formed a patchwork of familial bonds, but it was his own intellect and theological passion that would set him apart.

Richard married Catherine, a woman from Oundle, Northamptonshire, around the year 1627. Together, they raised ten children: John, Theodore, Jane, Martha, Susan, Samuel, Benjamin, Nathaniel, Anne, and Hannah. These children would extend the Resbury legacy into successive generations, but it was Richard's work, not his progeny, that cemented his name in the annals of biblical, puritan and reformed thought.

Richard Resbury's theological journey found its crux in his unflinching commitment to the doctrines of grace and the sovereignty of God. As a nonconformist minister, he served faithfully in Oundle, where his views stood firmly against the rising tide of the *gangrene* of Arminianism. Resbury's theological fire flared brightest during his written battles with John Goodwin, an influential Arminian preacher and theologian.

In 1651, Resbury published this current work in its original title: *Some Stop to the Gangrene of Arminianism*,[1] a pointed rebuttal of Goodwin's *Redemption Redeemed*. The title alone reflects Resbury's staunch Reformed stance, viewing Arminianism as a theological *infection* threatening the church's spiritual health. Goodwin, never one to back down from a quarrel, responded with *Confidence Dismounted*. Resbury's counter to this came swiftly in 1652 with *The Lightless Star, or Mr. John Goodwin Discovered a Pelagio-Socinian*. In this sharp-tongued work, Resbury accused Goodwin of resurrecting Pelagian and Socinian heresies, driving home his orthodox belief that Arminianism undermined God's sovereignty and man's utter dependence on grace.

---

[1] *Some Stop to the Gangrene of Arminianism, Lately Promoted by Mr. John Goodwin in his Book Entitled, Redemption Redeemed. OR, The Doctrine of Election & Reprobation in Six Sermons Opened and Cleared from the Old Pelagian and Late Arminian Errors*, by Richard Resbury, Minister of the Gospel in Oundle in Northamptonshire. (London, Printed for John Wright at the Kings-Head in the Old-Bailey, 1651).

Resbury's passion for doctrinal purity was not merely academic; it was personal and pastoral. As a minister, his teachings sought to *guard* his congregation against what he saw as the creeping dangers of *free will theology* and to anchor their faith in the unshakeable promises of divine election (a practice not many "reformed" ministers practice today).

In the twilight of his life, Resbury experienced the bitter cost of his convictions. Following his resignation as minister just six weeks before the *Great Ejection* on St. Bartholomew's Day in 1662, he retired to his home in Oundle. There, undeterred by the pressures of conformity, he practiced medicine and preached from his own household until his death around 1674.

Resbury was buried in Oundle, his life's work a testament to his theological rigor and unyielding devotion to God's sovereignty. His legacy, though contested in his time, endures as a steadfast witness to the Reformed faith in an age of great religious upheaval.

Other works:

THE Tabernacle OF GOD with MEN: OR, The Visible Church Reformed. A Discourse of the Matter and Discipline of the Visible Church, tending to REFORMATION. By Richard Resbury, Minister of the Word in Oundle, in Northamptonshire. (London, Printed in the year 1649).

The lightless-starre, or, Mr. John Goodwin discovered a Pelagio-Socinian and this by the examination of his preface to his book entitled Redemption Redeemed: together with an answer to his letter entituled Confidence Dismounted / by Richard Resbury...; hereunto is annexed a thesis of that reverend, pious and judicious divine, Doctor Preston ... concerning the irresistibility of converting grace. 1652.

THE SAINTS SUBMISSION TO THE WILL of GOD.
OR, A Sermon preached at the Funeral of a virtuous young Gentleman, Mr. WILLIAM ELMES, The only Son and Heir of THOMAS ELMES, of Warmington in the County of Northampton, Esquire. BY RICHARD RESBURY, Minister of Oundle. (LONDON, Printed by T. C. for J. Wright at the Kings Head in the Old-baily. 1654).

Paul's Soul Panting FOR A BETTER LIFE. A Sermon Preached at Lotherstock in the County of Northampton, Jan. 25, 1654. At the Funeral of that faithful Servant in Christ, Master John Bellamy, late Colonel of a Regiment of Foot, belonging to the famous City of London. With a brief Narration of his Life and Death. By RICHARD RESBURY, Minister of the Gospel at Owndle in Northamptonshire. (LONDON: Printed by R. I. and are to be sold by Tho. Newberry, at the three Lions in Cornhill, over against the Conduit. 1655.)

Richard Resbury Against Arminianism
By C. Matthew McMahon, Ph.D., Th.D.

The Rock of Divine Sovereignty

In the vast sweep of Christian history, few debates have burned as fiercely as those over God's sovereignty and man's will. It is a contest as old as Eden, as human as the heart's own *pride*. Richard Resbury, with the fervor of a prophet and the precision of a marksman, takes up the quill to challenge the Arminian camp—a theological school whose teachings on free will, election, and grace, he saw (*rightly*) as a dangerous affront to the majesty of God. Resbury's arguments, rooted in Scripture and braced with logic, call us to gaze beyond our frailty and into the infinite mind of the Creator. This is no easy task. His defense of predestination and reprobation is not only biblically faithful but spiritually essential.

The Sovereignty of God in Election: Romans 9 as the Axle of the Debate

Resbury, wielding the ninth chapter of Romans as a divine scalpel, sets out to dissect the assumptions of Arminianism. "For the children being not yet born, neither having done any good or evil, that the purpose of

God according to election might stand, not of works, but of him that calleth," (Romans 9:11). These words stand as the cornerstone of his argument, echoing through every syllable of his polemic. What Resbury understood, and what Arminianism so grievously misunderstood, is that election is not a reward but an act of pure mercy. God, like the potter shaping clay, chooses some vessels for honor and others for dishonor, not because of anything in the clay but because of His own *sovereign* will.

This doctrine cuts against the grain of human pride. *Prideful people* hate this doctrine. Arminianism, with its insistence that God's choice is conditioned upon foreseen faith, makes man the master of his own destiny, the captain of his soul. It is a theology that hums with the melody of humanism but strikes discordantly against the revelation of Scripture. Resbury would have none of it. He paints a vivid picture of humanity as clay in the hands of the divine Potter, emphasizing Paul's rhetorical question: "Shall the thing formed say to him that formed it, Why hast thou made me thus?" (Romans 9:20). Here is humility's lesson writ large. It is not ours to question God's sovereign decree but to submit and marvel at His wisdom. (See there, human pride *has* to be vanquished.)

The Necessity of Reprobation: The Other Side of Election

To modern ears, the doctrine of reprobation—that God actively ordains some to wrath—may sound harsh, even cruel. But for Resbury, it was a necessary corollary to election because *the Bible teaches it blatantly*. He leaned heavily on Paul's words: "What if God, willing to show his wrath, and to make his power known, endured with much longsuffering the vessels of wrath fitted to destruction," (Romans 9:22). These vessels, Resbury argued, are not mere accidents of history but deliberate actors in God's grand design. Their destruction serves to magnify God's justice, just as the salvation of the elect magnifies His mercy.

Arminians objected, crying out that such a decree makes God the author of sin. Resbury deftly parried this accusation, pointing out that God's ordaining of sin differs from His authorship of it. He permits sin to achieve His purposes without becoming its cause. This is not a capitulation to fatalism but an exaltation of divine sovereignty. As Resbury noted, if God's will could be frustrated by the will of man, He would cease to be God. The Almighty is not a spectator wringing His hands at human rebellion; He is the supreme ruler, turning even sin and Satan's schemes to His glory.

The Liberty of Man's Will: A Proper Understanding of Freedom

At the heart of Arminianism lies the idea that predestination robs man of his *free will*, making him a mere puppet. Resbury counters with the razor of distinction. Man's will, he argues, is free in that it chooses according to its *desires*, yet those desires are governed by God. Quoting Proverbs 21:1, "The king's heart is in the hand of the Lord, as the rivers of water: he turneth it whithersoever he will," Resbury demonstrates that God's sovereignty over the will does not destroy its freedom. It is God who moves the will, not by compulsion but by an inward inclination that aligns with His eternal purpose.

This divine orchestration preserves human responsibility. Resbury illustrated this truth by pointing to Joseph's brothers, who sold him into slavery out of malice. "But as for you, ye thought evil against me; but God meant it unto good," (Genesis 50:20). The brothers acted freely according to their sinful desires, yet their actions fulfilled God's plan. So it is with all human sin: freely chosen, yet sovereignly governed.

The Comfort of Election: A Fortress for the Soul

While critics of predestination often paint it as a cold and unfeeling doctrine, Resbury saw it as a wellspring of *Christian comfort*. "The election hath obtained it, and the rest were blinded," (Romans 11:7). These words, far from being a stumbling block, assure the believer that his salvation rests not on the shifting sands of his own efforts but on the unshakable rock of God's purpose. If salvation depended on human will, who could stand? Our wills are fickle, prone to wander, but God's will is steadfast and unchanging.

For the believer struggling with doubt, the doctrine of election offers assurance. If God has chosen us from eternity, nothing in time can separate us from His love. "Who shall lay any thing to the charge of God's elect? It is God that justifieth," (Romans 8:33). Resbury's words, steeped in the spirit of this text, call the anxious soul to rest in the knowledge that, "the gifts and calling of God are without repentance," (Romans 11:29). His electing love is not a fleeting whim but an eternal covenant.

A Theological Symphony: The Harmony of Sovereignty and Responsibility

Resbury's defense of predestination does not press the idea of fatalism but it is a directive towards *faith*. He understood that God's sovereignty and human responsibility are not enemies but friends. Paul, after unfolding the great mystery of election in Romans, does not conclude with apathy but with exhortation: "I beseech you therefore, brethren, by the mercies of God, that ye present your bodies a living sacrifice," (Romans 12:1). The elect are called to *holiness*, not because they fear losing their salvation but because they have been set apart for God's glory.

Arminianism, with its emphasis on *free will*, inevitably diminishes this call. If salvation ultimately depends on man's choice, then grace becomes a helper, not a savior. But Resbury reminds us that grace is sovereign. It does not merely assist the willing; it *creates* the willingness. "For it is God which worketh in you both to will and to do of his good pleasure," (Philippians 2:13). This grace does not destroy our humanity but redeems it, making us willing servants of King Jesus.

The Glory of God in Predestination

Richard Resbury's critique of Arminianism and his defense of predestination is not merely a theological exercise but an *act of worship*. His arguments, grounded in Scripture and steeped in humility, direct our gaze to the grandeur of God. In predestination, we see a God who is not contingent on His creation but who rules over all with wisdom and power. We see a God whose love for His elect is not fickle but eternal, not conditional but free.

In our age, as in Resbury's, the doctrine of predestination remains a stumbling block to human pride. It reminds us that we are not the masters of our fate, the captains of our souls. But it also reminds us that we are not left to ourselves. The same God who decrees our end also provides the means. He calls, justifies, and glorifies His people, ensuring that none are lost. This is no cruel tyranny but sovereign mercy, no grim determinism but divine love.

Let us then, with Resbury, bow before the sovereign Potter, acknowledging His right to shape us according to His will. Let us marvel at the wisdom of His decrees, even when they confound our reason. And let us rest in the assurance that, "all things work together for good to them that love God, to them who are the called according to his purpose," (Romans 8:28). In the doctrine of predestination, we find not only the justice of God but the riches of His mercy, not only the mystery of His will but the comfort of His grace. And in all these, we behold the glory of Christ the King, our great and sovereign Lord.

In Christ's grace and mercy,
C. Matthew McMahon, Ph.D., Th.D.
From My study, February, 2025
"...search the Scriptures..." (John 5:39).
www.apuritansmind.com
www.puritanpublications.com
www.gracechapeltn.com
www.reformedsynod.com

To the Reader

Reader,

You have here a small piece presented to your view, which has remained concealed with the author for over three years, as you may see by the *Imprimatur*. It might have stayed hidden had not those essential truths of God asserted in it—concerning His electing and redeeming grace, upon which His throne of glory is especially established, and wherein lies the treasured possession of His saints—been recently attacked by the audacious hand of that unfortunate man, Mr. John Goodwin, in his wretched treatise that he calls (but miscalls) "Redemption Redeemed." Firstly, my earnest prayer is, may the Lord rebuke him; and if that unique grace, which he presently so seriously despises and so boldly defies, should yet magnify itself in saving him, though as by fire, let the zeal of the Lord for His own most precious truth burn his work, for it is stubble. Indeed, whenever that grace shall truly visit him with the revelation of the truth as it is in Jesus, his own hands will eagerly pull down what he has built. Secondly, my hope and confident expectation is that the Spirit of the Lord will send forth faithful defenders of His truth, not only to confront him but to confound his doctrine, and for the good of His elect ones in this nation—those who, through weak judgment and lack of skill in the mystery of Christ, are susceptible to being led astray by such a spirit of error (only the foundation of God stands sure)—to disarm him as has already been done with his great masters Arminius and Corvinus, and the rest of that *troublesome* faculty. As far as I can discern (without partiality), he has not at all repaired their loss but, concealing it from common eyes, confidently treads in their well-worn steps, and to make his stance appear bold, challenges an entire university to refute him. (Surely such modesty and honesty must be the mark of the Spirit of Truth in him.) In the meantime, until a further antidote is prepared by a more skillful hand, I have ventured to offer this work that lay by me, if the Lord may bless it as a check to that spreading poison.

Let me say this: though it is not a direct answer to his book (for it was composed long before his discourse saw the light), it primarily focuses on the foundation of all—the decrees of God—endeavoring to clarify according to the Scripture (the only key to this mystery) the doctrine of election and reprobation. Once this is well established, his errors about the following doctrines, such as redemption and the perseverance of the saints, are struck at the root. Moreover, in discussing these decrees, the other controversial doctrines naturally come up; nor have I avoided the main objections usually made by the Arminian family regarding these doctrines. Thus, the substance of the entire controversy is addressed here. The best account I can give is to outline the order of the treatise, which is as follows:

In the first and second sermons, the doctrines of election and reprobation are discussed together, opening the ninth chapter of Romans, from verses 1 to 24, where the absolute decree is upheld. In the third sermon, the doctrine of election is treated separately, with absolute election further asserted. In the fourth sermon, the doctrine of reprobation is treated separately, with absolute reprobation proven. In the fifth sermon, those Scripture texts that are typically objected against the doctrines maintained in this discourse are clarified, examining the Arminian doctrines about the antecedent and consequent will, and the use of natural abilities for obtaining spiritual ends. In the sixth and final sermon, three other objections are answered: first, that which accuses the former doctrine of making God the author of sin; second, that which charges the same doctrine with portraying God as cruel, or at least not as merciful as the Scripture represents Him; third, that which accuses it of depriving man of the freedom of his will—indeed, this is the heart of the matter.

These objections are the knots I have singled out, not because I have an inflated opinion of myself or consider myself among the most capable of untying them—indeed, I am far below many of my brethren. But first, it is not fair to address a controversy while ignoring

To the Reader

the main objections. Second, I hope what is said here in response may be fruitful for the further establishment of some in the truth. Third, I wish to provide an opportunity for some scribe in our Israel, more thoroughly instructed in the Kingdom of Heaven, to bring out of his treasure things new and old, presenting these precious truths of God more clearly to His people. And now, I thank Mr. Goodwin, whose darkness, I am confident, will lead to more light; his boldness will encourage modesty. I will not say what kind of edge his sometimes, imperial dictates (instead of arguments, as is the Arminian style), his monstrous conclusions, his distorted quotations, his strange philosophy, and his consequent blasphemy will provoke in the spirits of those whom the Lord will honor to rescue His truth from his hands. I am only persuaded that the zeal of the Lord will accomplish it. This, along with a fruitful blessing upon it, shall be the earnest prayer of

Your servant in and for the truth,
RICHARD RESBURY.

The First Sermon

Romans 11:7, "But the election hath obtained it, and the rest were blinded."

The Apostle resumes the discourse he began in Romans 9, now drawing it toward a conclusion. To understand this passage, we must first note its occasion and then its content.

The Occasion

The Apostle addresses an objection arising from the Jews' rejection of the Gospel. In preaching justification by faith alone, apart from the works of the Law, he anticipates the following objection: If justification by faith is the only path to life, why have God's covenant people, the Jews, largely rejected it, clinging instead to the Law for righteousness? This leads to a further implication: If God's covenant with Abraham and his seed is valid, how can it be that He has seemingly cast off His people, Israel? This objection is introduced in verse 1: *"I say then, hath God cast away his people?"* The implied assumption is that God would not make void His covenant. From this, they conclude that justification by faith, as taught by the Apostle, cannot be true.

The Apostle's Response

The Apostle upholds the truth of the Gospel while addressing the objection in two parts:
1. He disclaims the idea that God has cast off His people (*"God forbid"*). God remains faithful to His covenant.
2. He refutes the objection:

First, he cites his own case: *"For I also am an Israelite,"* (verse 1), showing that God has not cast away all His people.

Second, he provides a distinction. God has not cast off any of His true covenant people, whom He foreknew. The key point is that among those outwardly within the covenant, some are foreknown by God as His own, while others are not. Those whom He foreknew are the true recipients of the covenant's eternal and spiritual blessings, and none of them are cast off. The rest, being merely outwardly associated with the covenant, were never truly His people. This distinction is summarized in verse 2: *"God hath not cast away his people which he foreknew."*

Note: If any of God's true covenant people could fall short of eternal life or abandon the truth, this would leave God guilty of breaking His covenant. The Apostle rejects such a notion, countering the false doctrine of the final apostasy of the saints.

Confirmation

The Apostle confirms his argument by recalling the state of the Church during Elijah's time (verses 2-5). Even when the nation as a whole fell into idolatry, God preserved a remnant who remained faithful. Applying this example to the present, he concludes that although the Jewish nation largely rejects the Gospel and incurs judgment, there is still a remnant chosen by grace who embrace the Gospel and find life.

In verse 6, he emphasizes that this election is entirely of grace, *excluding* works. Just as works have no role in justification, they have *no* role in election. Election is based solely on God's free favor, which precedes all time and cannot be influenced by foreseen works.

Verse 7: A Distinction in Israel

In verse 7, the Apostle distinguishes between the elect within Israel and the rest. He identifies the elect as the, "remnant according to the election of grace," (verse 5). The rest of Israel, hardened in their rejection, are contrasted with the elect. The term "hardened" (from the Greek πωρόω) implies a callous or impenetrable condition. This understanding aligns with John 12:40 and Mark 6:52, where the word is used to indicate spiritual insensitivity or stubbornness.

Observations from the Text

The First Sermon

1. **God's Sovereign Choice**: The difference between man *and* man originates in the sovereign will of God. Among His outwardly called people, some are foreknown with a peculiar love, while others are not.
2. **Eternal Outcomes**: Those chosen by God will certainly obtain eternal life: *"The election hath obtained it."* The rest are hardened unto death: *"And the rest were blinded."*

The Doctrine: *this text teaches that God, in His sovereign will, chooses some to eternal life while refusing others to death.* This distinction is grounded in God's purposes, not human merit.

Cautions in Handling the Doctrine
1. **The Mystery of God's Ways**: This doctrine touches on the deep mysteries of God, requiring reverence and humility. As the Apostle declares in Romans 11:33: *"O the depth of the riches both of the wisdom and knowledge of God!"* We must approach these truths with sobriety, seeking wisdom through prayer.
2. **Human Reason Resists**: Such doctrines often provoke human reasoning to *rebel*. For example, in Romans 9:14 and 19, God is accused of unrighteousness and tyranny. Here, we must set

aside our own understanding and follow Scripture's guidance, accepting God's revealed will even when it challenges our natural perceptions.

3. **Potential for Misuse**: This doctrine may be misused by some for licentiousness or murmuring against God. However, as the Apostle notes, the preaching of such truths has different effects: it opens the eyes of some while hardening others. Still, since God has revealed it in His Word, we are called to teach it with care.

4. **The Value of This Doctrine**: Properly understood, this doctrine brings great comfort, humility, and clarity to the Gospel. It magnifies the free grace of God and serves as a powerful defense against errors that oppose the truth.

5. **The Dual Effect of God's Word**: All truths of God produce different effects in different people. As Paul says, the Word is *"the savour of life unto life"* for some and *"of death unto death"* for others (2 Corinthians 2:16). Nonetheless, the truth must be preached for the nourishment of God's people, even if others misuse it.

This doctrine of election is therefore essential, both for *the glory of God* and the *comfort* of His people.

The doctrine presented here builds on the premise that the mysteries of election and reprobation are most fully addressed in Romans 9:1-24. The Apostle, in Romans 11, revisits these themes, drawing upon and expanding his previous arguments. Thus, to proceed, the Scriptures must first be explained, followed by a detailed consideration of the doctrines of election and reprobation. This approach ensures a foundation in Scripture and confirms the doctrine with additional testimonies as needed.

Romans 9 and the Jews' Rejection of the Gospel
The Apostle addresses an objection stemming from the Jews' general rejection of the Gospel. This rejection, alongside their resulting loss of eternal life, could be seen as a challenge to God's covenant with Abraham and his descendants. The objection has two parts:
1. The Jews' rejection of the Gospel is assumed as fact.
2. From this rejection, it is inferred that God has been unfaithful to His covenant.

The Apostle concedes the first point but denies the second.

The Jews' Rejection
In Romans 9:1-3, Paul expresses deep grief over the Jews' rejection of Christ. His lament shows both his personal love for his people and the seriousness of their condition. His wish to be, "accursed from Christ," for their sake (verse 3) reveals the depth of his love, akin to

Moses' intercession for Israel (Exodus 32:32). Though Paul could not take their place under God's wrath, his willingness reflects the mediator's heart, a shadow of Christ's ultimate sacrifice.

Paul's grief is heightened by the privileges God had given Israel (verses 4-5). These included their adoption, glory, covenants, law, service, promises, and the lineage of Christ. Despite such blessings, many Jews rejected the Gospel.

Denial of God's Unfaithfulness

In Romans 9:6, Paul denies that God's covenant has failed: *"Not as though the word of God hath taken none effect."* The covenant remains firm because it was never intended for all of Abraham's physical descendants. Paul provides three examples to demonstrate this distinction.

Three Examples Demonstrating the Covenant's True Heirs

1. Jacob's Posterity (Romans 9:6-7): Paul distinguishes between physical descent and covenantal inheritance: *"They are not all Israel, which are of Israel."* Here, "Israel" has a double meaning:
   - The first "Israel" refers to Jacob's physical descendants.
   - The second "Israel" refers to those spiritually chosen by God.

In this way, not all of Jacob's descendants are heirs of the covenant's spiritual blessings. Some have only an outward participation in the covenant, while others, the, "remnant according to the election of grace," inherit its eternal promises.

A *double sense* of being in covenant with God is highlighted:
1. Outward Covenant Membership: All of Jacob's descendants were outwardly part of the covenant, marked by circumcision and called to serve God.
2. Spiritual Covenant Membership: Only the elect, chosen by God, partake in the covenant's *ultimate blessings* of eternal life.

While many who are outwardly in the covenant may fall short due to unbelief, the true heirs, chosen by God, are preserved. God's *faithfulness* ensures their salvation.

2. Abraham's Posterity (Romans 9:7-9): Paul provides a second example, distinguishing between the natural and covenantal offspring of Abraham. Though all of Abraham's descendants were physically his, the covenant was specifically tied to Isaac: *"In Isaac shall thy seed be called."* This exclusion of Ishmael demonstrates that covenant blessings depend not on physical descent but on God's promise.

Paul explains that Isaac's birth itself was a result of God's promise, not natural strength (Genesis 18:10). Abraham and Sarah's bodies were "dead" in reproductive terms, and Isaac's birth was a miraculous fulfillment of God's covenant. Similarly, the true heirs of the covenant are those born of God's promise, not mere natural descendants.

3. Isaac's Family: Jacob and Esau (Romans 9:10-13): A third example arises in the distinction between Jacob and Esau, both sons of Isaac and Rebecca. This example strengthens Paul's argument by addressing potential objections to the previous instance.

Objections Addressed:
1. Isaac and Ishmael were born to different mothers (Sarah and Hagar), one free and one bond.
2. The promise to Sarah regarding Isaac came after Ishmael's birth.

Paul counters these objections by noting that Jacob and Esau were twins, sharing the same father and mother, yet God chose Jacob and rejected Esau. This choice occurred before their birth, confirming that it was not based on works or circumstances but solely on God's sovereign will: *"The elder shall serve the younger,"* (Genesis 25:23).

God's Love and Hatred: Paul refers to Malachi 1:2-3 to explain the distinction between Jacob and Esau: *"Jacob have I loved, but Esau have I hated."* This love and hatred signify God's eternal decree concerning their spiritual destinies—election to life for Jacob and reprobation to death for Esau. The desolation of Esau's inheritance is but an outward sign of God's eternal judgment.

The Ground of the Difference: God's Purpose (Romans 9:11)

Paul identifies the root of this difference in God's sovereign purpose. Before Jacob and Esau were born, and before they had done anything good or evil, God declared His choice: *"Not of works, but of him that calleth."*

- **Not Based on Works**: The difference was not based on any actions or merit, either foreseen or actual. The choice was entirely rooted in God's will.
- **Rooted in God's Purpose**: This purpose is described as "according to election," meaning God's eternal plan to save His chosen people. Election is God's gracious determination to grant life, while reprobation involves His sovereign decision to leave others in their sin.

Observations and Applications

1. **Eternal Life is the Covenant's Main Purpose**: The primary intention of the covenant is to grant eternal life.
2. **The Elect Obtain Eternal Life**: Those chosen by God to be heirs of the covenant will certainly receive eternal life.

3. **God Ensures the Fulfillment of Conditions**: The covenant not only promises life upon belief but also ensures that the elect will believe, as God grants them faith.
4. **God's Faithfulness Remains Intact**: Even though many outwardly associated with the covenant fall short of life, God's faithfulness is unshaken because the true heirs always obtain its blessings.

This teaching confirms the Apostle's denial of the objection that the Jews' rejection nullifies God's covenant. God's faithfulness is preserved because His election ensures the salvation of the true heirs of the covenant. How?

1. In defining the purpose of election, which, being a purpose of choice in regard to Jacob, must also include a purpose of *refusal* concerning Esau, this purpose of refusal is what constitutes reprobation.
2. Works are removed as the ground for their difference. Evil works are not the supreme cause of Esau's rejection, nor are good works the cause of Jacob's acceptance. Similarly, Esau's hatred and Jacob's love do not rest on any works of their own. Therefore, another ground must be found to explain Esau's condition, just as one must be identified for Jacob's condition. This ground can

only be what is implied about Esau through what is explicitly stated about Jacob.

3. The differing conditions of Jacob and Esau further illustrate this principle. If only the purpose of election had been in view, Jacob, as the beloved object, would suffice for the discussion. But the Apostle also mentions Esau as hated. By presenting this dual and opposing instance, the Apostle removes any imagined grounds in either Jacob or Esau themselves. Especially in Esau's case, he eliminates any possibility of a human cause for his rejection and instead attributes both Jacob's acceptance and Esau's rejection entirely to God's sovereign purpose. Thus, their differing conditions arise not from works, but from God. This distinction is based entirely on God's purpose of election and reprobation.

4. God's purpose of election regarding Jacob is such that it remains *unchanging*.

5. This purpose is "of God according to election," as of the one who calls. Through calling, we receive faith and the renewing work of the Spirit, which bring us into a state of life. Therefore, God's election includes granting faith and renewing the believer through the Holy Spirit, ensuring eternal life for the elect. This purpose depends on nothing in man, neither works nor foreseen

actions. It is entirely God's undertaking and provision.

It follows that when the Apostle excludes works, he excludes foreseen works as well as works already performed. Election is not of works but of God. If it depended on foreseen works, it would ultimately rest on human effort. God's purpose, however, cannot be based on anything other than Himself. It is unchangeable, having a foundation more secure than any foreseen work or quality in man. Thus, it is of God alone and by His sovereign will.

This excludes not only works but also foreseen faith. The Apostle does not say, "Not of works but of him that believeth," nor "Not of works but of him that justifieth," but instead, *"Not of works but of him that calleth."* Justification presupposes faith, and in calling, God grants faith. Therefore, election is not based on God foreseeing works or faith, but on His purpose to give faith. Foreknowledge of faith is not antecedent to God's purpose but is included within it, as it is His purpose to grant faith.

It becomes evident that the foreknowledge of evil works or anything in man is not the first cause of Esau's perishing. In Esau's case, evil works foreseen have no more bearing than evil works performed. This can be demonstrated through two conclusions:

1. The differing purposes of God—electing some and refusing others—are the primary cause of the differing states of humanity: those who embrace the truth and are saved, and those who reject the truth and are damned.
2. This purpose is not built upon anything in man. It does not stand or depend on human actions or qualities but is entirely independent and originates solely in God.

These conclusions are clearly supported by the Apostle's discourse and can be further confirmed.

First Conclusion: Jacob and Esau as Examples

The examples of Jacob and Esau are pivotal in addressing the broader question concerning the Jews. The Jewish nation largely rejected the Gospel and perished, while a remnant embraced it and obtained life. This distinction, first applied to Jacob and Esau, extends to *all* humanity.

Second Conclusion: Election and Reprobation Are Independent of Man

The Apostle presents election and reprobation as parallel and sovereign acts of God. Several arguments affirm this conclusion:

1. **God as First Cause:** All things that occur are either done directly by God or permitted by Him as the supreme ruler. Nothing happens apart

from His will. Augustine writes, "Nothing is done without the will of the Almighty that it should be done, He either suffering it to be done, or Himself doing it."[2] Even acts of sin, though they cling inseparably to human action, require God's *concurrence* in their occurrence. Otherwise, secondary causes would act independently of the first cause, making the creature *a creator*. God foresees all things as either ordained or permitted by His will, and His decree is the foundation of His foreknowledge. In this way, God's purpose precedes His foreknowledge in the order of nature.

2. **Knowledge of Possibilities and Certainties:** God knows all possibilities through His omnipotence and all certainties through His decree. Possible things are known in His power, while actual things are known in His purpose.

3. **God's Sovereignty in His Decrees:** If God's foreknowledge were independent of His decree, He would lose all liberty in determining His purposes. His decree would be bound by the creature's actions, rendering His will subordinate to human decisions. This undermines the sovereignty and supremacy of God, as His decrees would merely react to the

---

[2] *Enchrid. ad laurent.* c. 95.

creature rather than establish His eternal purposes.

The Glory of God in Election and Reprobation

1. **God's Glory as the Ultimate End:** All things exist for God's glory: *"For of him, and through him, and to him, are all things: to whom be glory for ever. Amen,"* (Romans 11:36). His glory is the ultimate goal of all His works, including election and reprobation. If His purposes were contingent on human actions, His glory would depend on the creature, undermining His sovereignty.

2. **God's Eternal Wisdom and Purpose:** The fall of Adam, the manifestation of justice, and the giving of Christ are not reactions to human actions but part of God's eternal plan to glorify Himself. Scripture reveals that God's glory is the ultimate aim of all creation and redemption.

God's purpose in the differing conditions of mankind—election and reprobation—is rooted *entirely* in His sovereign will and glory. It is independent of human actions, whether foreseen or performed, and encompasses all events leading to His ultimate goal. This purpose is revealed in His Word and confirmed through the Apostle's teaching.

The Second Sermon

Romans 11:7, "But the election hath obtained it, and the rest were hardened."

Verses 14–19: The Objection and Answer

The Apostle, knowing how human nature will endlessly dispute against this truth, anticipates and addresses an objection in verse 14: *"What shall we say then? Is there unrighteousness with God?"* This accusation arises from corrupt human reasoning against the doctrine of predestination.

The essence of the objection is this: If God deals unequally with those who are equal in themselves, then He must be unrighteous. According to the Apostle's teaching, human works, whether good or evil, are irrelevant as motives for God's decrees. Therefore, the accusation concludes, God must be unrighteous.

The Apostle's Answer

1. **Denouncing the Accusation:** The Apostle rejects this charge as blasphemous. Even if God deals unequally with those who are otherwise equal, such inequality does not constitute unrighteousness.

   Vindicating God's Righteousness in Election (Verses 15–16): The Apostle vindicates God's righteousness in election by pointing to God's sovereign liberty to show mercy as He pleases. He quotes Exodus 33:19: *"I will have mercy on whom I will have mercy, and I will have compassion on whom I will have compassion."* From this, the Apostle concludes: *"So then it is not of him that willeth, nor of him that runneth, but of God that sheweth mercy,"* (Romans 9:16). This demonstrates that neither human desire (*willeth*) nor effort (*runneth*) influences God's decree; His mercy arises solely from His will.

In Reprobation (Verses 17–18): Using Pharaoh as an example, the Apostle shows God's liberty in reprobation. He quotes Exodus 9:16: *"Even for this same purpose have I raised thee up, that I might shew my power in thee, and that my name might be declared throughout all the earth."*

Two key points emerge:
1. God raised Pharaoh up, encompassing his creation, preservation, elevation to power, and hardening in wickedness.
2. The purpose of this was to glorify God's name through Pharaoh's destruction.

The Apostle concludes in verse 18: *"Therefore hath he mercy on whom he will have mercy, and whom he will he hardeneth."* This affirms God's equal sovereignty in both election and reprobation.

Observations

1. **Human Resistance to Predestination:** *Human pride* resists the doctrine of predestination,

preferring to accuse God of unrighteousness rather than accept His sovereignty. This opposition has persisted throughout history—from the Pelagians in St. Augustine's time to Jesuits like Bellarmine and modern heretics who combine old errors against this truth.

2. **The Doctrine of Reprobation:** The Apostle addresses reprobation as well as election in the preceding verses, as evidenced by the objection that arises from both doctrines. His answer vindicates God in both cases.

3. **The Role of Works and Faith:** Neither good nor evil works, nor faith or unbelief, whether foreseen or performed, influence God's decree. If God's love for Jacob were based on foreseen faith or good works, and His hatred for Esau on foreseen unbelief or evil works, there would be no basis for the objection. God would then be dealing unequally with those who were unequal, not with those who were equal. Instead, God's decrees rest solely on His sovereign will.

4. **God's Will as the Standard of Justice:** Whatever God wills is *inherently* just, even when it surpasses our understanding of justice. The Apostle asserts that God's sovereign will to show mercy or harden is just, even though it arises above all considerations of human merit or demerit. Though we may not comprehend God's

righteousness in these matters, we must accept it because Scripture declares it.
5. **Comparative and Singular Predestination:**
    1. Comparative predestination refers to the difference between individuals like Jacob and Esau, where God's choice is based solely on His will.
    2. Singular predestination concerns the common qualification of all mankind: the universal corruption of nature. Some argue that predestination applies only to fallen humanity, not extending to creation and the fall.

Against this view, the Apostle's arguments show that God's decree arises *entirely* from Himself, *independent* of human conditions. The objection and answer in the text imply that predestination transcends both creation and the fall, considering man as uncreated in divine determination.

Arguments Against the View that Predestination Applies Only to Fallen Humanity
1. **The Objection:** If fallen, sinful humanity were the object of predestination, the objection loses its force. When all are equally deserving of condemnation, there would be no grounds to accuse God of unrighteousness for saving some and leaving others to perish.

2. **The Answer:** The Apostle's answer appeals to God's sovereign liberty, not to human sinfulness. If fallen humanity were the object, the Apostle could have answered more directly: since all deserve death, God is just in saving some and condemning others. Instead, the Apostle emphasizes God's sovereign will.
3. **The Context of the Apostle's Argument:** The Apostle's argument suggests that God's decree of predestination considers man as uncreated, preceding both the fall and creation. This continues the Apostle's earlier discourse, maintaining a consistent view of predestination.

Verse 19: A New Objection

"Thou wilt say then unto me, Why doth he yet find fault? For who hath resisted his will?"

This objection charges God with tyranny, questioning how He can fault and punish man for sin if He hardens them according to His will.

The Twofold Will of God

1. **Decreeing Will:** This refers to God's eternal purpose, by which He ordains all things.
2. **Declaring Will:** This is God's revealed will in Scripture, which commands obedience and forbids sin.

The Second Sermon

The Apostle's discourse demonstrates that God's decrees in election and reprobation are based entirely on His sovereign will. Human pride resists this doctrine, preferring to accuse God rather than acknowledge His supreme authority. God's justice is inseparable from His will, even when it surpasses human understanding. As Paul declares: *"Nay but, O man, who art thou that repliest against God?"* (Romans 9:20).

His decreeing will *determines* what shall be, while His declaring will *shows*: (1) what man's duty is, and (2) what God accepts when it is performed. Here, the Apostle speaks of God's decreeing will, which no one can resist. In contrast, God's declaring will is resisted whenever sin is committed. The objection arises because man, while resisting God's declaring will—what He commands and takes pleasure in—does not resist God's decreeing will. The objection, clearly stated, is this: If God has decreed that man shall sin and be hardened in his sins, and no one can resist this decree, how can He rightly punish man for his sin?

In response, the Apostle acknowledges the premise of the objection but denies its conclusion by appealing to God's absolute sovereignty over man. He argues for God's liberty to dispose of man entirely according to His will, which originates solely in Himself and not in anything within man. The Apostle rebukes man's insolence in contesting with his Creator, reminding him of God's dominion, which he illustrates

with the analogy of the potter and the clay (Romans 9:20-21).
1. The Potter Represents God.
2. The Clay Represents Mankind.
3. The Lump of Clay Represents Mankind Before Being Formed into Vessels.
4. The Same Lump Represents All of Mankind Equally Before God.
5. One Vessel Made for Honor and Another for Dishonor Represents One Man Created for Eternal Life and Another for Wrath.

From this objection and its answer, we must determine whether man fallen into sin or man not yet created is the object of predestination. This involves considering whether the sin of the first man (and the resulting corruption of all mankind) is accounted for *before* God's decree or is comprehended *within* it.

The objection presumes that men are hardened in sin according to God's decreeing will, a premise the Apostle does not deny but defends. Yet, does the consideration of sin in those to be hardened influence God's decree to harden them? Or is the sin for which they are hardened included within God's decree?

Answer: Although God foresees that they will sin before He hardens them, this foreseen sin does *not* precede His *decree* to harden. Instead, God's decree, rooted in His mere pleasure, determines: (1) to permit them to sin as a step toward hardening, and (2) to harden them in their sin as a step toward their condemnation.

1. If the decree to harden followed the foresight of sin, there would be no basis for the objection. It is universally accepted that God may justly harden individuals after they have sinned. Similarly, it follows that He may decree to harden individuals based on His foresight of their sin, without His decree being the cause of that sin. In this case, there would be no ground for accusing God of unrighteousness.
2. The Apostle's argument does not align with this view. The decree by which God wills the hardening of the reprobate is the same decree by which He hated Esau (Romans 9:13-19). This decree precedes all consideration of sin (Romans 9:11).

In this way, the sins for which the reprobate are hardened and condemned fall within God's *decree*. These sins are not merely foreseen apart from His decree but are decreed by Him with the intention of hardening the reprobate *for them*.

The next question is whether the natural corruption resulting from the fall of man is considered before God's decree. Does God decree to permit sin in response to fallen humanity already existing in sin? Or does His decree itself include humanity's fall and resulting corruption?

Answer: If the corruption of human nature were considered before God's decree, the objection would lose its force. It is universally accepted that God may justly leave fallen man in sin and may permit him to commit further sins, for which He can justly harden him and punish him with eternal wrath. If humanity's corruption were seen as preceding God's decree, there would be no basis for accusing Him of unrighteousness. So far, the objection supports the view that predestination concerns man as not yet created.

In his answer, the Apostle makes this even clearer. First, he appeals to God's absolute sovereignty over man by virtue of creation (Romans 9:20-21). Second, he clarifies God's purposes in creating man for specific ends—either for honor or dishonor (Romans 9:22-23).

1. God's absolute sovereignty is asserted in Romans 9:20: *"Nay but, O man, who art thou that repliest against God? Shall the thing formed say to him that formed it, Why hast thou made me thus?"* This establishes that God, as Creator, has complete dominion over man and is not obligated to explain His actions.
2. The sovereignty spoken of here applies to man as not yet created, not as already created or fallen. The Apostle's analogy of the potter and the clay

supports this. The potter has power over the same lump to make one vessel for honor and another for dishonor (Proverbs 16:4).

If the object of predestination were fallen man, the Apostle could have appealed to God's righteousness rather than His dominion, saying: Although God decrees to harden the reprobate, He first sees them as sinners apart from His decree. In this view, God decrees to: permit them to remain in their sinful state and multiply their transgressions. Harden them as a righteous judgment for their sins. This argument would have satisfied even the objector, as it is universally accepted that God is not obligated to rescue fallen humanity from sin. However, the Apostle emphasizes God's sovereign power rather than His justice, demonstrating that predestination concerns man as not yet created.

Cameron rightly observes that God's attributes are exercised in different ways: some (like mercy and justice) relate to objects already constituted, while others (like power and wisdom) concern the constitution of the object itself. Here, the Apostle emphasizes God's power, not His justice, as the basis of predestination. This power applies to man as to be created and to fall by God's decree, not to man already created or fallen.

This interpretation aligns with the Apostle's argument:

Romans 9:20 asks: *"Shall the thing formed say to him that formed it, Why hast thou made me thus?"* If fallen man were the object, the question would instead be: *"Shall the thing deformed say to him that formed it, Why hast thou marred me thus?"* The analogy of *the potter and the clay* assumes *one* undifferentiated lump, not separate and distinct lumps. Those who argue that faith or works foreseen determine predestination imagine two different lumps, while those who make fallen man the object deny the potter's power to make vessels for dishonor from any other lump than one already corrupt. In this way, from the objection and the answer, it is evident that predestination concerns man *as not yet created*. This conclusion is further supported by the argument from the angels, which we now consider.

The purpose of election and reprobation for the angels considers them as not yet created, or else it must be based on their works. One of these two must necessarily be the case because, unlike man, no fallen angel shares in the collective corruption and fall of the others. However, the idea that election or reprobation is based on works is to be denied for angels on the same grounds as it is denied for man. Those who concede that election and reprobation in humans are not of works yet insist that man as fallen is the object of predestination are at a loss to explain themselves here. If it is absurd to claim that human election or reprobation is based on works or faith (even *foreseen* works or faith), then the same absurdity applies to the case of angels.

If it can be granted without contradiction that angels are considered by God as to be created when He purposes their election or reprobation, then it must also be granted for man. Furthermore, the Scriptures support this view, though some, in attempting to avoid perceived contradictions, interpret them otherwise. Let us strengthen the doctrine of God's absolute power with another argument.

If, in a case of equal significance, God acts according to His absolute power, then it is no absurdity to grant the same here. This is evident, for instance, in the following:

1. The imputation of Adam's sin to all his posterity. By what standard of human justice am I, conceived thousands of years after Adam sinned, held accountable for *his* transgression? Would it be permissible between men that the offense of a father against his prince would condemn all his descendants to death, even those who were not yet born when the crime was committed? If such a covenant were established, by what right could it be made, and how could its fulfillment be considered more just than its abrogation?
2. The imputation of man's sin to Christ and, in Him, the punishment of all the sins of the elect. Could any earthly ruler execute the most

innocent and noble peer in his kingdom—indeed, the heir to his throne and the very child of his loins—in order to absolve a group of vile traitors? Yet, in God, this is most just, for He possesses absolute power over mankind and even over the human nature of Christ. The fact that Christ was willing to endure this punishment does not alter the matter in terms of justice, for as man, He was appointed and created by the Father for this purpose. If it had been possible for Christ as man to refuse this role, such a refusal would have been sin.

What, then, leads so many to insist that man as a corrupt mass is the object of predestination?

1. A false premise: Since election is a decree of mercy and reprobation a decree of justice, and since mercy saves and justice condemns fallen and sinful man, it is assumed that sin must be considered before the decree. Mercy and justice, it is argued, presuppose sin.

    Answer: The most that can be concluded from this is that God's decree determines that sin shall exist before either the salvation of the elect or the condemnation of the reprobate. It does not follow that God considers sin as something foreseen before His decree or that His foreknowledge of sin motivates the decree itself. For example, the decree of election is a decree to save all persevering believers, while reprobation is a decree to condemn all impenitent sinners. Salvation presupposes final perseverance in faith, and condemnation presupposes final impenitence in sin. However, the decree does not presuppose these conditions but comprehends and ordains them. Otherwise, election would be of works, with faith assuming the role of works, making the purpose dependent on the called rather than the caller, which contradicts the Apostle in Romans 9:11.

This mistake assumes that whatever is required for the execution of the decree must be foreseen apart from and prior to the decree as its motivation. In truth, the decree itself ordains whatever is necessary for its execution. For example, a man may resolve to leave a legacy through legitimate offspring. This purpose presupposes a wife. By this mistaken reasoning, the man must foresee having a wife before he resolves to leave a legacy, and this foresight must motivate his resolution. In reality, the man's resolution to leave a legacy leads him to resolve to take a wife. The decree that determines the end also comprehends the means to that end; otherwise, it would be a purpose without purpose.

Another error arises from the sequence of time: Since man's sin precedes his salvation or condemnation in time, it is thought that sin must also precede these intentions in the order of nature. God is said to glorify Himself in mercy and justice after considering sin.

However, the sin of man, as a means to God's glorification, is appointed in order to and by virtue of that end which God has preordained.

To clarify: What is first in God's intention is last in execution. A man may decide to build a house with specific dimensions and features for his own dwelling. His dwelling in the house is the last thing to occur, yet it was the first thing he intended. Similarly, God's intention to glorify Himself in man's salvation or condemnation *precedes* His intention to permit sin. Without the intention to permit sin, sin could not occur and therefore could not be foreseen. Thus, to claim that God foresees sin before decreeing to glorify Himself through man's salvation or condemnation leads to the *absurd* conclusion that man must first be condemned or saved and only then permitted to sin.

To conclude: Election is a decree of mercy, and reprobation is a decree of justice. Yet both are acts of absolute and arbitrary power, favoring or refusing purely at God's pleasure.

However, God's justice can be understood in two ways:
1. Toward Himself: This justice compels God to act according to His wisdom for His own glory.
2. Toward the creature: This justice disposes good or evil upon the creature under certain conditions.

In the first sense, election and reprobation are acts of justice, as God is to be justified in all He does according to His wisdom for His glory. In the second sense, they pertain more to mercy and justice as dispositions.

Another obstacle is a misplaced fear of making God the author of sin by asserting that He decreed and willed Adam's fall.

Answer: To be the author of sin is to act in such a way as to incur guilt. Guilt presupposes subjection to a law. Show any law that God violates by decreeing that man shall sin. Does God will Adam's fall? How then?

1. Is it against His will? He is omnipotent.
2. Is it without His knowledge? He is omniscient.
3. Is it beside His will? Not a single hair falls from the head, nor a sparrow to the ground, nor does a lot fall in the lap apart from God's will. If Adam's fall was beside God's will, then God did not determine man's purpose in creation, nor the end of angels, nor His glory in the administration of human and angelic history, nor the gift of Christ, nor the Gospel. This would render the entire economy of redemption and all of creation subject to chance. Such a view is no better than believing that the universe arose from the random collision of atoms.

In the first sermon on Romans 9:11, we laid out three arguments proving that God's purpose arises solely from Himself. These arguments also fully demonstrate that both the sin of Adam and all other sins are decreed by God. Let us now apply them specifically to this issue.

God Decrees to Permit Sin. If God did not decree to permit sin, He could not even foresee it. As previously shown, without a decree, God's foreknowledge would imply that new plans arise in His mind as time unfolds, which is inconsistent with His nature. If God permits sin in time, He must have willed from eternity to permit it. Thus, He decrees that sin shall occur under His permission.

The permission of sin cannot be an end in itself, as if it were limited to the mere act of permitting. Rather, the permission of sin necessarily involves its occurrence under that permission. Every sinful act comprises two elements: the act itself, which is good as a work of creation, and the sin, which cleaves to the act. God, as the first cause and fountain of all being and goodness, brings about the act itself, while permitting the sin that adheres to it.

This is evident in several biblical examples: the sale of Joseph by his brothers, the crucifixion of Christ, and the afflictions of Job. In each case, God's will and hand are acknowledged. If God had not willed the crucifixion of Christ—the greatest sin ever committed—how could He have willed the salvation of mankind through Christ, a plan He purposed from eternity (Ephesians 1:4)? Similarly, if God had not willed Adam's fall—the origin of all sin—how could He have willed human redemption through Christ, which begins with that fall?

God *Wills Ends* That Necessitate Sin. If God wills an end that cannot be achieved without sin, He also wills that sin will occur. God wills to glorify Himself through the display of His sparing mercy in Christ's salvation of some and His revenging justice in the condemnation of others. This display of mercy and justice presupposes sin, for there can be no mercy or justice without sin. Therefore, God wills sin to exist, including the first sin, without which none of the others would follow.

It Is Good That Sin Exists for God's Glory. Although sin is evil, the existence of sin serves the greater good of God's glory, as it is necessary for the manifestation of His attributes. Thus, while God does not approve of sin itself, He approves of its existence, as a means to fulfill His eternal purpose. Augustine writes: "It is not to be doubted that God does well even in allowing evil to be done. For He permits evil by a righteous judgment, and everything righteous is good. Therefore, while evil itself is not good, the existence of both good and evil is good, as it serves God's purposes."

This distinction allows us to understand that sin's existence is decreed by God without implying that He approves of sin as an act. Sin is against His approving will but within His decreeing will.

God's Liberty in His Decrees. When God permits sin—whether the first sin or any subsequent sin—it is by His free decree. To deny this would imply that God's will is determined by the actions of His creatures, which contradicts His sovereignty. If God did not freely decree sin, His will would be dependent on external motives, which is incompatible with His perfection.

To deny this would also suggest that God is *not* perfectly happy, for perfect happiness requires that all things, even evil, occur *according to His will*. It is better for all things to align with His will than for anything to exist outside of it. Thus, God wills even those things He does not approve, approving their existence for His glory.

Objection: Did God Create Man to Damn Him?

The Scriptures do not shy away from expressions like *"The LORD hath made all things for himself: yea, even the wicked for the day of evil,"* (Proverbs 16:4) and *"vessels of wrath fitted to destruction,"* (Romans 9:22). However, such phrases do not mean that God wills the damnation of the wicked *as an end in itself*. God does not take pleasure in the condemnation of sinners for its own sake. Rather, He wills the condemnation of the reprobate for the sake of His glory.

God's purpose in creating and permitting sin includes His intention to glorify Himself in two ways:
1. By displaying His mercy and justice in saving some.
2. By displaying His revenging justice in condemning others.

In this way, God decrees to create man, to permit sin, to save some from sin, and to harden others in sin, all as means to His ultimate end—the manifestation of His glory. The condemnation of the wicked is not the primary end but part of the means to achieve God's ultimate purpose. When it is said that God made the wicked for the day of evil, it is also said that He made all things for Himself (Proverbs 16:4). Similarly, *"vessels of wrath fitted to destruction,"* are so described in the context of God's intention to display His wrath and power (Romans 9:22).

The Apostle's Explanation: Supreme Ends and Righteous Execution

The Apostle in Romans 9:22-23 presents the supreme ends of God's decrees:
- *"What if God, willing to show his wrath, and to make his power known, endured with much longsuffering the vessels of wrath fitted to destruction,"* (Romans 9:22).

- "And that he might make known the riches of his glory on the vessels of mercy, which he had afore prepared unto glory," (Romans 9:23).

These verses reveal God's purposes in decreeing sin and salvation: the display of His wrath and power and the manifestation of His glory and mercy.

While the decree of God arises above the creation and fall of man, the Apostle justifies it by appealing to the ends God has set for Himself—His glory. God's glory is the ultimate end of all things (Romans 11:36). As all things are from Him, so all things are directed to Him. The universe as a whole reflects God's majesty, displaying His wisdom, power, holiness, mercy, and justice. This is what theologians call the "good of the universe"—the *resplendence* of God's majesty in His works.

God decrees to glorify Himself in His justice and mercy. This decree also displays His power and dominion over His creatures. Just as the potter has authority over the clay to make one vessel for honor and another for dishonor, so God's dominion over humanity is unquestionable. The objection that vessels of wrath are fitted for destruction by their own actions misses the point: their condition is also part of God's sovereign plan (Proverbs 16:4).

Righteous Execution of the Decree

God does not condemn without cause. The reprobate are condemned only for their sin. Although God decrees the end, He executes this decree in a manner consistent with His righteousness. He endures their sin with much longsuffering and *condemns them* only when they *condemn themselves*. Thus, God's sovereignty governs the decree, while His righteousness governs its execution. His decree is absolute, arising from His sovereign will, yet its execution is regular, punishing sin in accordance with justice.

The reprobate are condemned for sin alone, and their condemnation fulfills God's purpose to glorify His justice. Thus, even as we explore this great mystery of divine decrees, the Apostle's teaching reveals the consistency and glory of God's eternal plan.

The Third Sermon

Romans 11:7, "But the election hath obtained it, and the rest were hardened."

Let us proceed to confirm the doctrine:
  1. For the part that pertains to election.
  2. For the part that pertains to reprobation.

  1. Concerning Election. Election may be described as the eternal decree of God, by which He has, out of pure love and good pleasure, ordained certain individuals—those who are the fewest in number—to eternal life and to all blessings that lead to life in Christ, to the praise of His glorious grace.

  From this description, we note the following points:
  1. Election is the purpose or decree of God.
  2. It is His eternal decree.
  3. It pertains to eternal life.
  4. It concerns specific persons—a certain and determined number singled out by name.
  5. It applies to the fewest of men.
  6. It arises from God's love and good pleasure.
  7. It is based solely on His love and arbitrary pleasure, without any regard to man's merits.
  8. It includes, not only eternal life, but all blessings in Christ that lead to life.
  9. It is effectual, accomplishing its purpose.
  10. It is for the praise of God's glorious grace.

The Third Sermon

Election as God's Purpose or Decree. The Scriptures use two words to describe this:

1. *Prothesis* (πρόθεσις), meaning "purpose"—a plan set down beforehand (Romans 9:11; Romans 8:28). It is called "His purpose" and "the counsel of His will" (Ephesians 1:11).
2. *Proorizo* (προορίζω), meaning "predestination"—a predetermined plan that sets certain boundaries within which some will receive blessings that others will not (Ephesians 1:5, 11; Romans 8:29). This eternal distinction and separation of men for their final state originates here.

2. Election as Eternal. If election is a decree, it must be an eternal act of God, as nothing new arises in Him, though new things proceed from Him. This is clearly affirmed in Scripture: *"He hath chosen us in him before the foundation of the world,"* (Ephesians 1:4). The kingdom prepared for the elect was established, *"from the foundation of the world,"* (Matthew 25:34). Christ was foreordained as their Redeemer, *"before the foundation of the world,"* (1 Peter 1:20).

3. Election for Eternal Life. The Jesuit Stapleton, and some others even among us, argue that the Apostle's discussion of election in Romans 9 concerns temporal blessings like the inheritance of Canaan or the birthright, rather than eternal life. They claim that God's love for Jacob and hatred for Esau pertain to their descendants' earthly privileges.

However, it is clear that election pertains to eternal life:

1. The objection raised in Romans 9 centers on the Jews' *rejection* of the Gospel and their *loss* of eternal life. The Apostle's argument assumes this context.
2. Paul distinguishes between the elect and the reprobate within the families of Jacob, Abraham, and Isaac, attributing this difference to God's eternal decree.
3. The example of Pharaoh, with his hardening, points to eternal condemnation. This is reinforced by the conclusion that the reprobate are, *"vessels of wrath fitted to destruction,"* (Romans 9:22) and the elect are, *"vessels of mercy prepared unto glory,"* (Romans 9:23).
4. Paul applies the doctrine of election to both Jews and Gentiles, emphasizing eternal salvation rather than temporal privileges. The elect obtain *"salvation"* (Romans 11:11), *"reconciliation"* (Romans 11:15), and *"eternal life"* through the Gospel.

4. Election Concerning Specific Persons. Election pertains to specific individuals, a determined number chosen by name in God's eternal counsel.
1. Paul's discourse in Romans 9 demonstrates this, showing that the difference between those who receive or reject the Gospel arises *from God's decree*. Jacob and Esau are examples of this distinction, which results in the calling of some to life and the hardening of others to death.

2. Election is often referred to as being written in the "book of life." This metaphor does not describe a law or general pathway to life but a register of those specifically chosen for life.
3. The particular details of election confirm this point.

Objection to Revelation 3:5. Some argue that Revelation 3:5 suggests election is changeable, as it mentions names being blotted out of the book of life.

Answer: Election's unchangeable nature will be discussed fully later. For now, note that such expressions are anthropomorphic, reflecting human understanding. To blot a name out of the book of life means to deny eternal life to a person or to reveal that their name was never truly written there. Similar language is used in Matthew 13:12, where Jesus says, *"Whosoever hath not, from him shall be taken away even that he hath."* This means only that it will become evident that what they appeared to have, they did not truly possess.

Election is called the "book of life," indicating it pertains to eternal life. The elect are said to have their names written in heaven. Furthermore, the land of Canaan and other temporal blessings were outward symbols of the eternal inheritance (Hebrews 11:9-10). The Apostle's discussion of Esau's subjection to Jacob in Romans 9 reflects their spiritual states concerning eternal life. Esau's despising of his birthright (Genesis 25:32) signifies his spiritual rejection and servitude.

From the Apostle's teaching in Romans 9, it is clear that election and reprobation concern eternal life and death. This truth is affirmed by the metaphor of the "book of life," which registers the heirs of eternal life, and by the consistent testimony of Scripture. Let us now move to the following particulars to examine each aspect of this doctrine more thoroughly.

Election Pertains to the Fewest of Men. If election is not of persons but merely of a general way to life (as some suggest, claiming it decrees only that believers shall be saved and unbelievers damned, without determining who shall believe or disbelieve), then it does not apply to the fewest or the most but *either* to all equally or none equally.

Election Is of Love and Good Pleasure. Election arises from God's love and good pleasure, which inherently relate to specific persons. As stated, *"Jacob have I loved,"* (Romans 9:13), this love reflects a personal singling out. If election were merely a decree establishing the terms or way of salvation, it would have no place for such love, as it would not pertain to individual persons.

Election Arises from Mere Love and Arbitrary Pleasure. This love and pleasure are not contingent on any distinctions in persons, whether existing or foreseen. Election is not based on any merits or qualities in individuals, but solely on God's sovereign choice.

Election Includes Eternal Life and All Blessings Leading to Life. The faith, holiness, and all other graces granted to those who are saved depend upon this decree and are fruits of it. Thus, the decree must first choose the persons to whom these blessings are given. Because God has set these individuals apart in love, He bestows upon them the graces necessary for eternal life.

Election Is Effectual for Eternal Life. This decree is not dependent on human obedience to God's call or perseverance, but rather, by virtue *of the decree*, individuals are effectually brought to obedience and perseverance.

Election Magnifies the Glory of Divine Grace. God *makes* vessels of honor; He *does not find them as such*. They are prepared beforehand in His eternal counsel for glory. This preparation highlights God's sovereign work in creating the conditions for their salvation, underscoring that the choice is entirely His.

Arguments Confirming These Truths

Election Pertains to the Fewest of Men. This concept, often resisted by human reasoning, is explicitly affirmed in Scripture. *"Many are called, but few are chosen,"* (Matthew 20:16). Comparing those who are outwardly called with those who are not; the vast majority of humanity was overlooked for much of history. For the first 4,000 years, the world as a whole was left without the outward call of the Gospel (Acts 17:30). God allowed the nations to walk in ignorance while revealing His will only to certain families, such as Seth's line and later the descendants of Abraham (Psalm 147:19).

Even in the Gospel era, many nations remain without the Word of God. Yet all the elect are called, typically through an outward call, which often extends to their children in the covenant. Beyond this, they are inwardly and effectually called, justified, and ultimately glorified (Romans 8:30). Among those outwardly called, many remain unsaved; only a remnant is inwardly and effectually called. Paul affirms, *"There is a remnant according to the election of grace,"* (Romans 11:5).

Election is of Love and Good Pleasure. The words *"Jacob have I loved,"* (Romans 9:13) and *"according to the good pleasure of his will,"* (Ephesians 1:5, 9) reveal God's love as the foundation of election. This love involves singling out individuals for life. In Scripture, to "know" often signifies to love: *"After that ye have known God, or rather are known of God,"* (Galatians 4:9). Likewise, *"The Lord knoweth the way of the righteous,"* (Psalm 1:6), but He declares to the wicked, *"I never knew you,"* (Matthew 7:23). Election, therefore, is a decree of distinguishing love. It is a love that embraces some while rejecting others, limiting His grace to those He has purposed to save.

Election is of Mere Love and Absolute Pleasure. It is neither based on good works nor on faith foreseen. This is evident from Romans 9:11, where Paul states that God's election stands, *"not of works, but of him that calleth."* It is through God's effectual call that the elect receive faith and the renewing work of the Holy Spirit. This call is the unchangeable foundation of eternal life, rooted in God's sovereign purpose, which depends on nothing in man.

The Apostle makes clear that no divine purpose depends on anything outside of God. As demonstrated in the first and second sermons, predestination arises above all considerations of the creature, including sin. Man is not considered as fallen or even created but solely as subject to God's sovereign will.

Election Reflects God's Sovereign Dispensations. God's dealings with humanity reveal His absolute sovereignty. Why did He choose the Jews as the sole nation of His covenant, leaving the rest of the world in ignorance for so long? It was not because He foresaw greater worthiness in them (Deuteronomy 9:4-5). Why does He send the Gospel to some nations and not to others? Why was the mystery of salvation through Christ revealed at a specific time after being hidden for ages (Romans 16:25-26)? The only answer is: *"Even so, Father, for so it seemed good in thy sight,"* (Matthew 11:26).

Election is of Grace, Not Works. Paul declares, *"Even so then at this present time also there is a remnant according to the election of grace. And if by grace, then is it no more of works,"* (Romans 11:5-6). If election is not of works, it cannot be of works foreseen, as election is an eternal purpose, preceding any human action. Faith foreseen would similarly qualify as a work, making God's purpose dependent on man, contrary to Paul's teaching.

Faith and Works Do Not Precede Election. If faith or works foreseen influenced God's choice, grace would no longer be free. Yet Scripture repeatedly emphasizes that salvation is by grace, not by works, to prevent human boasting (2 Timothy 1:9; Ephesians 2:8). If foreseen faith or works played a role, God's free gift would be undermined, and human effort would take precedence over divine grace.

Election Is Clearly Evident in Christ. Christ, the head of the elect, exemplifies God's sovereign choice. What merit could be foreseen in the human nature of Christ to move God to exalt Him as the head of angels, the only begotten Son of God, and the Savior of the world? None. Augustine rightly observes that in Christ's election, we see the clearest evidence of God's free and sovereign choice.[3]

Election Includes All Spiritual Blessings in Christ. In Romans 8:29-30, Paul traces the entire chain of salvation to election: *"Whom he did predestinate, them he also called: and whom he called, them he also justified: and whom he justified, them he also glorified."* Similarly, Ephesians 1:3-11 attributes all spiritual blessings—holiness, adoption, redemption, forgiveness, and eternal inheritance—to God's electing purpose. These blessings are freely given in Christ, entirely apart from human merit. Through election, God assigns to His chosen people all things necessary for life and godliness, demonstrating that salvation is entirely of His sovereign grace.

---

[3] Lib. *de. predest. sanct.* c. 8.

Objection: We are elected in Christ, but we are in Christ only by faith. Therefore, our faith foreseen is the cause of our election.

Answer: We will explain the true meaning: We are elected in Christ, meaning we are elected to receive, in Him, all blessings prepared for us through our election, as members united to Him as the head. Christ is not the reason or motive for God's decree but, the means by which the decree is accomplished. As the Apostle states, *"For God hath not appointed us to wrath, but to obtain salvation by our Lord Jesus Christ,"* (1 Thessalonians 5:9). We confirm that this understanding is correct.

Christ Himself as Ordained by Election as Mediator of the New Covenant: In Romans 4:16, the Apostle shows that God, in designing the covenant of grace, made Christ its *head* and *mediator* with a special regard to the elect seed. This seed comprises *all* who are assured of the covenant for life. Therefore, Christ was ordained as mediator not as the reason for the decree but for the sake of those to whom God decreed eternal life.

Faith is Given by Election, Not Foreseen as Existing Independently: Faith, through which we might be considered in Christ and represented to God, is a gift of election. It is not foreseen in us independently but determined by God's decree to grant it. *"And as many as were ordained to eternal life believed,"* (Acts 13:48). Jesus confirms this truth: *"But ye believe not, because ye are not of my sheep,"* (John

10:26). Those who are Christ's sheep hear His voice and believe because they were already His sheep according to election, even before their calling. As Paul writes, *"According to the faith of God's elect,"* (Titus 1:1). Faith, holiness, and all graces depend on this decree.

Faith cannot precede the decree since all holiness and obedience flow from election.

We have previously seen that holiness depends on predestination, as Ephesians 1:4 states, *"That we should be holy and without blame before him in love."* Otherwise, it would imply that we choose God in Christ before He chooses us, which contradicts *"Ye have not chosen me, but I have chosen you,"* (John 15:16). This would also contradict Paul's teaching in Romans 9:11 that election is *"not of works."* From this, we understand that texts such as 2 Thessalonians 2:13 (*"God hath from the beginning chosen you to salvation through sanctification of the Spirit"*) and 1 Peter 1:2 (*"Elect according to the foreknowledge of God the Father, through sanctification of the Spirit"*) mean that we are chosen unto salvation, and sanctification is one of the means decreed for achieving that end. This further demonstrates that election pertains to specific persons and is absolute.

Election is Effectual Unto Life. Not one of God's elect will finally perish. Every one of them will certainly attain eternal life.

Election is Immutable: The purpose of election is firm and unchangeable. Paul declares, *"The foundation of God standeth sure, having this seal, The Lord knoweth them that are his,"* (2

Timothy 2:19). Election's foundation is God's unchanging will: *"The immutability of his counsel,"* (Hebrews 6:17).

The Elect are Preserved from Falling: Though the elect may, before their call, be children of wrath (Ephesians 2:3) or afterward face weaknesses and temptations, they are preserved by God's unchangeable election.

Effectual Calling: Every one of the elect *will*, in due time, be effectually called to salvation. *"All that the Father giveth me shall come to me; and him that cometh to me I will in no wise cast out,"* (John 6:37). They are first given to Christ by the Father through election, and then redeemed by Him. Their being Christ's sheep is due to their election, not their faith: *"Ye believe not, because ye are not of my sheep,"* (John 10:26). Everyone given by the Father will certainly come to Christ and receive eternal life. This effectual call is clearly taught in John 6:44-45: No one can come to Christ unless drawn by the Father. All who are drawn will come. All who come will receive eternal life, as Jesus promises: *"I will raise him up at the last day,"* (John 6:44). The Father's drawing is an inward, heart-transforming teaching. *"Every man therefore that hath heard, and hath learned of the Father, cometh unto me,"* (John 6:45). Augustine observes, *"If every man that hath learned of the Father comes, then he who comes not hath not learned."*[4]

Final Perseverance: Those taught and drawn by the Father will certainly persevere. Jesus states that all who

---

[4] Lib. *de predest. sanct.* c. 8.

come to Him will be raised up to glory: *"This is the Father's will which hath sent me, that of all which he hath given me I should lose nothing, but should raise it up again at the last day,"* (John 6:39).

Only the Elect are Given the Power to Come to Christ: Those who do not come lack the power to do so. Jesus declares, *"No man can come to me, except the Father which hath sent me draw him,"* (John 6:44). Those who are drawn come, and those who come are given eternal life. Consequently: all who are drawn by the Father will come. All who have the power to come are drawn. Since not all come, not all are drawn or have the power to come. Only the elect, those given by the Father to Christ, are drawn and given the ability to come. Therefore, they alone are brought to salvation.

Objection: *John 17:12* is used to argue that some given by the Father to Christ, according to election, may perish.

Answer: This interpretation contradicts verse 2 of the same chapter, as well as John 6:37 and the related passages we have already examined. The form of speech in John 17:12 does not necessarily infer that Judas was given by the Father in the sense of election. Similar forms of speech are often exceptive in wording but exclusive in meaning. For example, Matthew 12:4 states, *"It was not lawful for him to eat, neither for them which were with him, but only for the priests."* This might sound as if some of David's companions were priests, but the true meaning is that it was unlawful for anyone except the priests to eat the showbread. Similarly, in John

17:12, the meaning is: none of those the Father has given to Christ shall perish, and Judas, as the son of perdition, was not one of those given.

Even if Judas were considered given by the Father, this refers to a different kind of giving than that based on eternal election: Judas was given outwardly, as are all who are outwardly called and profess Christ, though few of them are chosen. Judas was given, in regard to his apostolic office, as mentioned in John 6:70: *"Have not I chosen you twelve, and one of you is a devil?"* But concerning the eternal election tied to salvation, Christ expressly excludes Judas in John 13:18: *"I speak not of you all: I know whom I have chosen."*

Effectual Calling and Perseverance
1. All the elect will, in due time, be effectually called.
2. After their calling, they will be upheld by grace against all temptations, ensuring they persevere to eternal life.

The same Scriptures that prove effectual calling also confirm the elect's certain perseverance to life. To these, we add 2 Timothy 2:19, Matthew 24:24, Revelation 13:8, Revelation 17:8, Revelation 20:15, and Romans 8:33-34. These passages demonstrate that the firm foundation of life and perseverance in grace is grounded in election. Not one of God's elect will fall short of eternal life. The covenant of grace was specifically designed with the elect in view, ensuring life for them: *"Therefore it is of faith, that it might be by grace; to the end the promise might be sure to all the seed,"* (Romans 4:16).

Errors in Arminian Doctrine

From the doctrine of election, we discern several erroneous teachings in the Arminian view: the uncertainty of a called person's spiritual and final condition. The uncertainty or impossibility of God's foreknowledge regarding that condition. The concept of temporary election and reprobation.

1. Uncertainty of the Spiritual Condition: Arminians argue that God cannot determine a sinner's will by the work of the Holy Spirit without infringing on human freedom. They claim that the liberty of the will requires that a sinner may resist or embrace the call of God, and after receiving grace, may or may not persevere. This makes salvation entirely uncertain—whether any person might be saved, whether the Church Militant or Triumphant might exist, or whether Christ's incarnation, suffering, and death might ultimately prove fruitless.

2. Denial of Foreknowledge: Arminians hold that since salvation depends on human choice and will—whether to embrace or reject God's call—God does not decree how any particular person will respond. They argue that human liberty requires an undetermined outcome, making foreknowledge of such undetermined events impossible. To claim certainty in foreknowledge without certainty in the event is contradictory. Some Arminians evade this problem, while others deny God's foreknowledge outright.

3. **Temporary Election and Reprobation:** Arminians teach that election is contingent on foreseen faith and perseverance, while reprobation is based on foreseen unbelief and obstinacy. Consequently, election and reprobation cannot be eternal. Instead, they must occur only when faith or unbelief manifests in a person's life. However, if God's foreknowledge of such conditions is denied, as their doctrine necessitates, election and reprobation can only occur in real time. This makes election temporary and revocable. Arminius himself speaks of an external act of reprobation, and his followers suggest that election is not eternal, that it is revocable, and that individuals can move between being elect and reprobate.

The Glory of Divine Grace in Election

The true doctrine of election, as revealed in Scripture, exalts the glory of God's grace:

1. **Election Grants Great Blessings in Christ:** These blessings include the greatest of all gifts—Christ Himself, as well as all spiritual blessings in Him (Ephesians 1:3-6).
2. **Election is Effectual Unto Salvation:** Election guarantees the fulfillment of God's purpose, just as the completion of the Temple elicited shouts of *"Grace, grace unto it,"* (Zechariah 4:7). The ultimate accomplishment of salvation leads to eternal

admiration of God's glory, as Paul states: *"When he shall come to be glorified in his saints, and to be admired in all them that believe,"* (2 Thessalonians 1:10).

3. **Election is Freely Bestowed:** It is not based on works or faith but entirely on God's call, as Paul writes: *"Who hath saved us, and called us with an holy calling, not according to our works, but according to his own purpose and grace,"* (2 Timothy 1:9).

4. **Election is Peculiar to the Elect:** It includes some while excluding others, accompanied by the decree of reprobation (Romans 9:22-23). This distinction is profoundly moving to the believer: *"Why did God set His love upon me and choose me for life, while rejecting so many others?"*

Those who advocate universal grace and redemption, denying the particularity of election, *undermine* the glory of God's grace and fail to understand its true depth and purpose. Their doctrine may seem wise in their own eyes, but it betrays ignorance of the divine grace they claim to uphold.

The Fourth Sermon

Romans 11:7, "But the rest were hardened."

We now turn to the decree of reprobation.
1. **Definition of the Term:** Reprobation is the opposite of election, as seen in Isaiah 41:9.
2. **Nature of Reprobation:** It can be understood by considering the doctrine of election and from explicit Scriptures concerning reprobation.

Reprobation *is the eternal decree of God whereby He, solely by His will, has hated the rest of humanity apart from His elect.* He has ordained them to dishonor and eternal destruction through their sins, for the display of His sovereign power, the glory of His revenging justice, and the demonstration of His mercy upon the saved.

This definition will be evident as we examine it, in light of prior discussions, so we will proceed concisely.
1. **The Existence of Reprobation:** A decree opposite to election is clear from Romans 9:11, as proved in the first sermon through three arguments when explaining this verse. It is further supported in the second sermon's exposition of Romans 9:14-18 and by the second observation therein.
2. **The Nature of Hatred in Reprobation:** This hatred, contrasted with God's electing love, is evident in Romans 9:13: *"Jacob have I loved, but Esau have I hated."*

This hatred involves exclusion from the covenant of life and eternal death, as established in the first and third sermons when examining Romans 9:10-13.

Let us now examine three aspects: 1. What this hatred entails. 2. The objects of this hatred. 3. The basis for this hatred.

1. The Nature of God's Hatred in Reprobation. God's hatred manifests in two aspects:

1. A decree permitting sin to occur in the reprobate, leading to their hardening in it.
2. A decree of hardening them in sin, leading to their condemnation.

God decrees sin's existence in the world, as previously demonstrated in the second sermon. This sin exists only by His permission, without which it could not occur. However, regarding the reprobate, God decrees both the permission of sin for their hardening and their hardening in sin for their eventual condemnation.

In Romans 9:18, Paul declares: *"Therefore hath he mercy on whom he will have mercy, and whom he will he hardeneth."* This refers to God's love for Jacob and His hatred for Esau, highlighting the honor and glory bestowed on the elect (Romans 9:21, 23) while showing wrath and power against the reprobate (Romans 9:22). Similarly, Romans 11:7 states: *"The election hath obtained it, and the rest were hardened."*

While sin is common to both elect and reprobate, its purpose differs. In the elect, sin becomes the avenue for redemption through Christ. In the reprobate, sin leads to hardening and eternal condemnation. Thus, God's love for the elect is evident in their calling and perseverance, while His hatred for the reprobate is evident in their abandonment to sin and ultimate hardening.

2. What Is Hardening in Sin? Hardening is God's righteous judgment upon sinners. It involves God withdrawing His grace, allowing them to fall entirely under the sway of their lusts and Satan's dominion. They become incapable of spiritual good and grow *worse*, even when confronted with the most powerful means against sin.

There are two types of hardening: 1. **A temporary hardening:** This occurred in Christ's disciples (Mark 6:52) and resulted in dullness of understanding. 2. **A final hardening:** This is peculiar to the reprobate and manifests as stubbornness against God, exemplified in Pharaoh, who continually resisted God despite witnessing His mighty works (Exodus 9:17). The hardened state involves blindness to spiritual truth and obstinacy against God's commands, as seen in Isaiah 6:9-10 and Matthew 13:14-15.

3. How Does God Harden the Reprobate? 1. **By *giving them over* to their lusts:** God withdraws the enlightening, restraining, and convicting influences of His Spirit, allowing them to plunge headlong into sin. For a time, reprobates may seem close to salvation, experiencing the work of the Spirit, yet they *resist*. In response, God ceases to restrain them, permitting them to follow their corrupt desires. This is why Scripture attributes their hardening to both God (*e.g.,* John 12:40, Romans 1:24) and themselves (*e.g.,*

Matthew 13:15). Pharaoh, for instance, is described as both hardening his heart and having his heart hardened by God.

2. By giving them over to Satan's dominion: Reprobates, having chosen to serve Satan rather than God, are subjected to Satan's power. God uses Satan as an instrument of judgment, blinding their minds further and stirring greater enmity toward God. This is evident in 2 Thessalonians 2:10-12, where those who reject the truth are handed over to Satan's *delusions*. Similarly, 1 Samuel 16:14-19 describes an evil spirit from the Lord tormenting Saul. While the spirit comes *from the Lord* in judgment, it is Satan who acts as God's agent.

As the Supreme Mover: God actively sustains the reprobate in their actions, even as they act sinfully. For instance, in Psalm 105:25, God is said to turn the hearts of the Egyptians to *hate* His people. While God moves them, He remains sinless, as He merely permits them to act according to *their own wicked desires*.

The immediate cause of hardening is the sinner's *own rebellion*. God's decree of permitting sin and hardening in sin precedes all foreseen or committed sin. However, the execution of this decree follows actual sin, as seen in 2 Thessalonians 2:10-12: *"Because they received not the love of the truth... God shall send them strong delusion, that they should believe a lie."* Similarly, Romans 1:24-26 shows God giving sinners over to their lusts due to their idolatry and rebellion.

The reprobate are described as vessels of dishonor and wrath, fitted for destruction (Romans 9:21-22). Some are appointed to wrath, as Paul notes in 1 Thessalonians 5:9: *"For God hath not appointed us to wrath, but to obtain salvation by our Lord Jesus Christ."* The implication is clear: while the elect are appointed to salvation, others are appointed to wrath. Jude 4 refers to certain men as *"ordained to this condemnation."* Just as election is the book of life, reprobation is the book of death, with the names of the reprobate written for destruction.

The objection that Jude 4 refers only to Enoch's prophecy (verse 14) is invalid. The fore-writing mentioned here signifies God's eternal decree concerning the reprobate, just as election signifies His decree concerning the elect.

The Fourth Sermon

Romans 11:7, "But the rest were hardened."

We continue by addressing the doctrine of reprobation.

Evidence from Enoch's Prophecy: The question arises: How does it appear that Enoch's prophecy was written? Since Jude speaks of men in his time being prophesied about by Enoch so many generations earlier, it follows that they were appointed to judgment *ages before*. If so many ages prior, then logically, this appointment must have been decreed from all eternity. There is no reason to suggest that God would suddenly decree it in Enoch's age, apart from the eternal nature of all His decrees. His love in election and His hatred in reprobation are not based on any works foreseen or performed by man.

This is supported by 1 Peter 2:8: *"And a stone of stumbling, and a rock of offence, even to them which stumble at the word, being disobedient: whereunto also they were appointed."* Similarly, Proverbs 16:4 states: *"The LORD hath made all things for himself: yea, even the wicked for the day of evil."* God, in creating humanity, had the condemnation of the reprobate in view for His own glory. Thus, reprobates are vessels of dishonor and destruction formed by God, as taught in Romans 9:20-22.

We have demonstrated that there is indeed such a decree of divine hatred regarding the reprobates and clarified its nature.

2. The Objects of God's Hatred. Who are these reprobates? **Answer:** All who are not elect. The apostle writes: *"The election hath obtained it, and the rest were hardened,"* referring initially to the Jews. Yet in the broader context, Paul divides all of humanity into these two categories, as previously noted in the second sermon (Romans 9:14-19). Since God has chosen some, and only some, to life, it follows that He has determined all the rest to death. To claim otherwise would require positing a group of people for whom God has made no determination, either for life or death. But if no determination is made: God has not decided how He will be glorified through them. Their eternal state is left undecided. Their earthly course and end are undetermined. Such a notion undermines God's providence and contradicts His role as the universal and supreme ruler over all creation.

The decree of reprobation has already been proven. Since there is no biblical evidence or logical reason to limit reprobation to only some of the non-elect, it must apply to all who are not elect. In election, God prepares life and all blessings leading to it. All things depend on election for God's glory. Since all humanity is ultimately saved or damned, it follows that all but the elect are reprobate. Revelation 20:15 makes clear that condemnation at the final judgment derives ultimately from non-election. This demonstrates that eternal life depends entirely on election, just as Habakkuk 1:12 suggests concerning God's eternal purposes. Few, if any, who admit the reprobation of some would deny its application to all but the elect.

3. The Basis for God's Hatred. Why does God decree that the non-elect will be permitted to sin, hardened in sin, and condemned for sin? **Answer:** There is no basis for this decree except *His will for His glory*. As the apostle Paul states, God hates merely *because He wills*: Paul explicitly removes human works from consideration, attributing everything to God's purpose (Romans 9:11). He resolves the distinction between the elect and the reprobate entirely to *God's will* (Romans 9:15-24). For a fuller explanation, refer to the exposition of Romans 9:11 in the first sermon and the extended discussion in the second sermon (Romans 9:14-22). These passages demonstrate: 1. Three arguments proving that God's purpose is entirely self-determined. 2. The apostle's discourse in addressing and refuting objections from Romans 9:14-22, which confirms the same. Thus, reprobation is God's eternal decree of hatred. It involves permitting sin for the purpose of hardening, hardening for the purpose of condemnation, and applies to all except the elect.

The ultimate purpose of reprobation is God's glory: **1. In His Sovereign Power:** God exercises absolute authority over humanity, considered neither pure nor impure but as yet uncreated. His decree ordains all but the elect to sin and destruction by sin (Romans 9:20-21). This sovereignty is discussed in the second sermon, where Paul's defense of God's absolute power (Romans 9:20-21) was thoroughly explained. **2. In His Just Wrath:** God's justice is glorified in His wrath upon perishing sinners. Romans 9:22 states: *"What if God, willing to shew his wrath, and to make his power known, endured with much longsuffering the vessels of wrath fitted to destruction?"* The power referenced here (Greek: *dynamis*) refers to God's might in executing judgment upon the reprobate. This differs from the power mentioned in Romans 9:21 (Greek: *exousia*), which refers to God's *authority* as Creator to determine man's final state. As the potter shapes vessels for honorable or dishonorable use, so God ordains humanity's destiny. The reprobate, as vessels of wrath, are fitted for destruction. While they bring destruction upon themselves by their sins, their creation was ordained with their ultimate condemnation in view. This aligns with Proverbs 16:4: *"The LORD hath made all things for himself: yea, even the wicked for the day of evil."*

In His Mercy Toward the Elect: Romans 9:23 highlights God's purpose in demonstrating *"the riches of his glory on the vessels of mercy, which he had afore prepared unto glory."* This was previously discussed at the conclusion of the third sermon, under the description of election as being to the praise of His glorious grace. Thus, God's decree of reprobation serves to glorify His sovereign power, just wrath, and abundant mercy. These attributes are fully displayed in His eternal purpose, as Paul teaches in Romans 9:22-23.

The Fifth Sermon

Romans 11:7, "But the rest were hardened."

Having expounded the doctrine of reprobation, we now address objections raised against it. These objections are of two kinds: Express texts of Scripture. Arguments that allege great absurdities in the doctrine.

1. Texts of Scripture. The passages most commonly cited by opponents include: *"Who will have all men to be saved, and to come unto the knowledge of the truth,"* (1 Timothy 2:4). *"The Lord is not willing that any should perish, but that all should come to repentance,"* (2 Peter 3:9). *"As I live, saith the Lord GOD, I have no pleasure in the death of the wicked; but that the wicked turn from his way and live,"* (Ezekiel 33:11). *"Have I any pleasure at all that the wicked should die? saith the Lord GOD: and not that he should return from his ways, and live?"* (Ezekiel 18:23). *"For I have no pleasure in the death of him that dieth, saith the Lord GOD: wherefore turn yourselves, and live ye,"* (Ezekiel 18:32). These texts are frequently emphasized, with the argument being that God declares:

1. Positively, that He wills all to be saved.
2. Negatively, that He does not desire anyone to perish.
3. That God expresses His desire for their salvation by calling them to repentance, affirming that He has no pleasure in their death, not even in the death of those who perish, and He swears this by His own life.

Answering These Objections. We provide: 1. General answers to these Scriptures collectively. 2. Specific responses to each individually.

Scripture Must Be Interpreted Harmoniously: We have already established from Scripture that God hates some individuals in view of their condemnation. This hatred involves His decree to permit sin leading to hardening and His decree to harden them in sin leading to condemnation. This decree is independent of any merit or action on man's part, yet it regards sin as, the means by which condemnation is carried out. As the potter forms vessels from the same lump of clay, making some for honor and others for dishonor, so God, from humanity equally represented before Him, decrees to make some vessels of mercy for glory and others, vessels of wrath for destruction (Romans 9:11-23). The differing decrees of election and reprobation are the ultimate causes of the spiritual and eternal conditions of individuals: *"The election hath obtained it, and the rest were hardened,"* (Romans 11:7).

God's will is sovereign: *"I will have mercy on whom I will have mercy, and whom I will I harden,"* (Romans 9:18). Some were ordained to condemnation (Jude 4). God made all things for Himself, even the wicked for the day of evil (Proverbs 16:4). Some are appointed to stumble at Christ and His Word, being disobedient (1 Peter 2:8). These are contrasted with the elect, described as a chosen people (1 Peter 2:9). Thus, Scripture must be interpreted in a way that reconciles these texts with those objections raised.

Distinguishing God's Will: God's will is understood in two senses: **His Decreeing Will:** This refers to God's eternal purpose or intention, determining what shall or shall not happen. *"But our God is in the heavens: he hath done whatsoever he hath pleased,"* (Psalm 115:3). *"For who hath resisted his will?"* (Romans 9:19). Whatever God decrees comes to pass, and whatever does not happen was not decreed by Him. His decreeing will cannot be frustrated, for even the rebellious wills of men and devils ultimately fulfill it. Augustine observes: *"To will or to nill is so in the liberty of Him who wills or nills, that neither can His will be hindered nor His power overcome."*[5]

His Declaring Will: This refers to God's revealed commands, which express what is pleasing to Him and what He approves or disapproves of. It is reflected in God's commands and His provision of means, often expressed in language suited to human understanding. For example, when God commands Abraham to offer Isaac, His declaring will expressed Abraham's duty and tested his obedience, but His decreeing will did not intend Isaac's death, as revealed in the final outcome. This declaring will often does not align with the actual event, as it was God's decreeing will that Abraham not sacrifice Isaac.

Thus, God's declaring will can be resisted and frustrated, as seen when His commands are broken or His provided means are rejected: *"O Jerusalem, Jerusalem... how often*

---

[5] Lib. de *Corrept. & grat.* c. 14.

would I have gathered thy children together, even as a hen gathereth her chickens under her wings, and ye would not!" (Matthew 23:37). When God is said to will all to be saved, or none to perish, this either refers to: 1. The scope of His declaring will, in which salvation is made available to all through commands and means, though not all receive it. 2. A specific distinction within His will, as discussed below.

Specific Responses to the Texts. Limiting Universality: When Scripture speaks of "all," the term must often be understood in a limited sense, not as an absolute universality. For instance, when Paul says God desires all to be saved (1 Timothy 2:4), the context shows he refers to people of all ranks and classes, not every individual universally.

Distinction of God's Will: When Scripture says God is not willing that any should perish (2 Peter 3:9), this speaks to His declaring will, which sets forth His approval of repentance and faith. However, His decreeing will determines who will actually come to repentance and faith.

God's Sovereignty in Salvation: The idea that God genuinely desires the salvation of all but cannot accomplish it undermines His sovereignty. If God's will to save all is taken as His decreeing will, then all would be saved, for "*whatsoever the LORD pleased, that did he in heaven, and in earth, in the seas, and all deep places,*" (Psalm 135:6).

Objections Against God's Sovereignty Addressed. is God's Will Frustrated? If God truly wills the salvation of all and possesses the power to achieve it, then all would be saved. To suggest otherwise implies either weakness in God's power or inconsistency in His will.

Does God Change? If God first willed all to be saved but later willed otherwise, this implies change in His nature, which is impossible: *"For I am the LORD, I change not,"* (Malachi 3:6).

Natural Inclination vs. Determined Will: Some argue that God's will for universal salvation is a natural inclination rather than a determined purpose. However, this is inconsistent with His nature as a perfect, pure act, in whom there is no incomplete or latent inclination.

God's Glory in Election and Reprobation. The salvation of the elect and the condemnation of the reprobate serve God's ultimate purpose: His glory. If God wills the salvation of all but *allows* some to perish for His greater glory, then it cannot be said He *genuinely wills* universal salvation. His decrees always align with His glory, which is the measure and end of all His works. Thus, there is no contradiction within God, for His will is one, perfect, and harmonious.

From the Happiness of God. If God is perfectly happy, then whatever He wills must come to pass. Happiness is an entire and perfect good, and it is more fulfilling to possess all that one wills than to lack it. If lacking something willed does not diminish happiness, then lacking more would not either; by that logic, lacking everything willed would not diminish happiness at all. This reasoning would absurdly suggest that one could be as happy with none of their desires fulfilled as with all of them, which common sense utterly rejects.

From the Knowledge of God. If God knew from eternity who would be condemned, then He must have willed their condemnation beforehand, as His knowledge of their fate flows from His will. Whatever He knows as something that will occur, He knows either in itself or in Himself. He cannot know it in itself before it exists, for before creation, only God existed. Thus, God must know it in Himself, meaning He knows *it in His will*.

Objection: But just as we see what is present in certain moments of time, God, in His eternity, comprehends all time at once. Since His eternity is the full possession of a boundless life at once, He sees everything in time as if it were present.

Answer: For God to see anything in itself during eternity requires that the thing itself coexists with His boundless life. Just as a man cannot see something in a moment of time that does not yet exist, God cannot see anything in itself before all time that has not yet come into being. Otherwise, He would see time in itself before time existed, which is a contradiction. This limitation does not indicate imperfection in God but rather an impossibility in the thing itself.

Furthermore, the causes of things, which are themselves created, cannot be seen in themselves before time since they, too, exist only in time. Therefore, whatever

God knows from eternity as destined to occur, He knows in Himself and through His will.

God's Threefold Knowledge
1. **Apprehension of Nature:** In God, there is an apprehension of the nature of all things, similar to how humans conceive ideas in their minds. For example, a builder may imagine a house without yet deciding whether it shall or shall not be built. Thus, God apprehends all possibilities—both what can and cannot occur.
2. **Knowledge of Possibility:** God knows what is possible because it lies within His power to make it so. However, this does not determine what shall occur, as God is capable of far more than He actualizes.
3. **Knowledge of What Shall Be:** God's knowledge of what shall be is grounded in His will. Before creation, God could have conceived of infinite possible worlds, yet He knew this world would be created because He willed it so. Similarly, God knew from eternity who would not be saved because He willed it to be so.

The Arminians falter regarding God's knowledge of man's eternal state, admitting no determinate basis for it in either God or man. 1 Timothy 2:4, *"Who will have all men to be saved, and to come unto the knowledge of the truth."* 2 Peter 3:9, *"The Lord is... not willing that any should perish, but that all should come to repentance.*" In these verses, the argument is made that God wills all to be saved and none to perish. However, this must be understood as referring to God's *declaring* will—not His decreeing will—because:

1. **Denial of Means:** God does not provide all people with the necessary means for salvation. For the first 4,000 years, the majority of the world was left without the knowledge of the covenant of grace, which was confined to the church, first among the patriarchs and then among the nation of Israel. Even now, many nations remain without the Gospel.
2. **Denial of the Spirit:** Even among those who receive the means of grace, many are denied the Spirit, which alone makes those means effective.

Example from Scripture: Jesus testified that Tyre and Sidon would have repented if they had witnessed the miracles performed in Capernaum. Yet the means of grace were withheld from them (Matthew 11:21).

Objection: All in Adam were taken into the covenant of grace.

Answer: If true, this still does not explain why Adam's posterity would come to saving knowledge solely because of his covenant standing. It is false because Christ, not Adam, is the root of Gospel righteousness (Romans 5).

Objection: Ancestors lost the means of grace for themselves and their descendants.

Answer: Even if granted, this does not prove that God willed their descendants to receive saving knowledge.

The Fifth Sermon

Many nations never received the Gospel at all, even long after Christ's resurrection.

Objection: The natural world offers sufficient initial revelation, which, if properly used, would lead to Gospel knowledge.

Answer: This view, held by Jesuits and refuted even by some Roman Catholics, is false for several reasons:

1. **God's Sovereign Mercy:** God reveals Himself to those who do not seek Him (Romans 10:20).
2. **Grace is Unmerited:** Salvation depends on God's mercy, not human effort or will (Romans 9:16).
3. **Divine Sovereignty:** God has mercy on whom He wills and hardens whom He wills (Romans 9:18).
4. **Human Distinction is From God:** *"Who maketh thee to differ? and what hast thou that thou didst not receive?"* (1 Corinthians 4:7).
5. **Unlikely Recipients of Grace:** God often calls the most sinful and morally corrupt individuals, while leaving behind those seemingly better qualified.

Augustine's Observation: "Should I try to judge God's election by my reasoning, I might favor those of greater intelligence or lesser sinfulness. Yet God confounds my reasoning by choosing the weak to shame the strong and the foolish to shame the wise."[6]

Preventing Grace. This doctrine denies the possibility of human works preceding grace. If man's natural

---

[6] *Ad Simplic. Lib. 1. ad finem fere.*

effort could merit saving grace, then grace would be a debt, not a gift. Grace, by definition, cannot be earned by works. Therefore, the idea that natural abilities could lead to salvation overthrows the very concept of grace.

Objection: It is by the merits of Christ, and therefore it is of grace.

Answer: The Apostle declares that if it is by works, then it is not of grace. Therefore, asserting this view undermines grace just as much as claiming we are justified by works. Both render grace meaningless. As for the text in Romans 10:18, compared with Psalm 19, it is utterly absurd to interpret it as implying universal redemption. The passage plainly refers to the Apostles and other sent teachers preaching the Gospel to human ears. Faith comes directly from hearing their message, as explained in verses 14–17. It does not refer to the Sun, Moon, and stars proclaiming God's works to human eyes, which might at most prepare men remotely for the Gospel. Furthermore, what is said in Psalm 19 is allegorical, likening the Gospel's spread through the Apostles to the Sun's course across the heavens.

The Denial of the Spirit's Saving Operation. While many enjoy the external means of salvation, the Spirit's saving work is not granted to all. The same Gospel message can be, "the savor of life unto life" for one person and "the savor of death unto death," for another (2 Corinthians 2:16). Some are converted, while others are hardened.

The Fifth Sermon

1. **God Makes the Difference:** It is God who creates the difference between individuals. "For who maketh thee to differ? and what hast thou that thou didst not receive?" (1 Corinthians 4:7). Conversion, saving illumination, faith, and repentance are all gifts from God (Ephesians 1:17; 2:8; Philippians 1:29; 2 Timothy 2:25; Ezekiel 36:26-27).
2. **It is Entirely by Grace:** This grace is granted without regard to any prior works (2 Timothy 1:9; Romans 11:5-6; Romans 9:11).
3. **God Exercises Absolute Sovereignty:** "The wind bloweth where it listeth," (John 3:8).
4. **God Provides Both Power and Action:** God not only grants the power to come to Him but also *ensures* its exercise. Without the Father's drawing and teaching, no one can come (John 6:44-45). Where this work is absent, there is no ability to come; where it is present, the sinner both can and *does* come.
5. **God Acts According to His Decree:** Some are converted because of God's decree, while others are hardened against the very means of salvation (Romans 9:18; Acts 13:48; Romans 8:30; Ephesians 1:4-5). The Jews, for instance, were not converted by Christ's powerful ministry because God had long determined their hardening, as Isaiah prophesied (Isaiah 6:9-10; John 12:37-42).

The claim that God's will refers to everyone without exception is untenable. Even His declaring will—providing the means of salvation—is not extended universally. Far less does His decreeing will, which determines both the means and their application, apply to all. St. Augustine observes: "God could turn the will of the wicked to good—He could, for He is omnipotent. Why does He not? Because He does not will to. Why He wills not, is with Himself (*penes ipsum est*). We should not seek to be wise beyond what is fitting."[7] Attempting to explore God's sovereignty and wisdom in this matter is futile; one who strains to comprehend it will lose their sight, their depth, and their understanding. Such mysteries belong to God alone.

Answering Specific Texts. 1 Timothy 2:4, "*Who will have all men to be saved, and to come unto the knowledge of the truth.*" The context makes it clear that this refers to all ranks and orders of men—kings, rulers, and subjects alike. During Paul's time, kings and rulers were often great persecutors of the Gospel. It might seem futile to pray for such hostile individuals, but Paul asserts that God has His elect among every class, including rulers. This parallels Galatians 3:28, where no distinction of nation, sex, or condition excludes anyone from salvation in Christ.

2 Peter 3:9, "*The Lord is not slack concerning his promise... not willing that any should perish, but that all should come to*

---

[7] Lib. 6 de Genes. ad literam. c. 15. "The will of God is the necessity of things."

repentance." The Apostle writes "to us-ward." Who are these? Peter was an elect believer writing to dispersed Jews who were likewise elect believers (1 Peter 1:1-2; 2 Peter 3:1). Therefore, the passage means that God delays judgment to gather all His elect. He is not willing that any of His elect should perish. This also points forward to the great ingathering of Jewish believers in their eventual restoration (Romans 11:28-32).

Ezekiel 33:11 and Ezekiel 18:23, 32 and God's Declaring Will: God does not delight in their death in the sense that He commands them to repent and provides them with means to do so. **Decreeing Will:** God wills their death not as a tyrant but as a righteous judge. Their condemnation glorifies His power and justice. The Jews charged God with injustice, claiming He punished them for their fathers' sins (Ezekiel 18:2). They also accused Him of unmercifulness, suggesting He was unwilling to forgive repentant sinners (Ezekiel 18:23, 33:10, 17). God's response clarifies that He does not will their death in the sense of unjust punishment or refusing repentance. Instead, their destruction is for their own guilt and for His glory.

Universal Redemption Misinterpreted. Many Scriptures alleged in favor of universal redemption are misunderstood and misapplied. Proper interpretation requires:

1. **Contextual Reading:** Many of the main texts cited for universal redemption, when read with their context, do not support such claims.

2. **The Analogy of Faith:** Fundamental doctrines, such as predestination, anchor us against the error of universal redemption. Those properly instructed in this doctrine are safeguarded from such misunderstandings.

Clarifying Ezekiel's Texts

The primary context of Ezekiel 18 and 33 is not eternal condemnation but temporal judgments. In Ezekiel 18:2 and Jeremiah 27:27-31, the issue is the Jews' suffering under the desolation of their land. They complain that God is unjust, punishing them for their fathers' sins, while justifying themselves as undeserving victims.

God's response is twofold: **They Are the Cause of Their Own Misery:** Their suffering is a result of their own actions, not God's injustice. **Repentance is Still an Option:** God calls them to turn from their iniquities, offering them life *if* they obey. Arminians misuse these texts, interpreting them as addressing eternal damnation while ignoring their clear focus on temporal judgments. Their arguments are built on misinterpretations and irrelevant applications, distracting from the true message of these Scriptures.

The Sixth Sermon

Romans 11:7, "The election hath obtained it, and the rest were hardened."

We now address objections raised against the doctrine of reprobation, which, if true, they claim would either accuse God or excuse man.

Objection 1: According to this doctrine, God must be the author of sin, and therefore guilty of it. This objection is based on three grounds: 1. God decrees sin, and this decree necessitates man's sinning. 2. God acts in sin, as the first cause producing actions to which sin is inseparably attached. 3. God denied Adam the grace necessary for him to persevere in righteousness, making his fall inevitable.

Answer: The foundational claims of this objection are admitted as true: that God decrees sin, acts in sinful actions, and denied Adam perseverance. However, the conclusion—that God is the author of sin—is entirely false and without basis.

1. Concerning God's Decree of Sin. God's Decree of Sin: It has already been established that God decrees the existence of sin. However, this decree does not make God the author of sin, because the decree is an internal act within God and does not directly impose anything upon the creature. Internal acts of God do not place anything in the object.

The Necessity of Sin: The decree of God creates a necessity for sin, but it is not an absolute or compulsive necessity. It is a conditional necessity—a necessity of consequence. Since God has decreed it, it cannot fail to happen. Yet, man sins freely, choosing to sin without compulsion or natural necessity.

Similar Necessity from Foreknowledge: If God foreknows that man will sin, it must necessarily happen, or else God's foreknowledge would be false. Therefore, we must either admit this conditional necessity or deny God's foreknowledge entirely.

God's Necessity: If man sins without God's decree, God Himself would be subjected to a conditional necessity of foreknowing man's sin or reacting to it, without liberty to prevent it. By rejecting God's decree, we diminish God's freedom and subject Him to man's actions.

2. Concerning God's Acting in Sin. God as the First Cause: Scripture teaches that God, as the Creator, is the first cause of all motion in His creatures. "In him we live, and move, and have our being," (Acts 17:28). As He is the source of life and existence, so He is the source of motion. Without His sustaining and moving power, nothing could act. The dependence of all creation on God for motion can be likened to the wheels described in Ezekiel 1:16. The motion of the inner wheel is encompassed and governed by the motion of the outer wheel. Similarly, God's motion governs and produces all actions within creation.

God Governs the Wills of Men: Scripture affirms that God turns the hearts of men as He wills. "The preparations of the heart in man, and the answer of the tongue, is from the Lord," (Proverbs 16:1). "The king's heart is in the hand of the Lord... he turneth it whithersoever he will," (Proverbs 21:1). He turned the Egyptians' hearts to favor Israel (Exodus 11:3), and later turned their hearts to hate His people (Psalm 105:25).

Duties Arising from God's Sovereignty Over the Heart. Seek God: Recognize that all your motions depend on Him, and surrender yourself to His will. **Glorify God:** Acknowledge Him as the sovereign ruler of all your ways (Daniel 5:23). **Heed His Spirit:** Respond to His inward workings in fear and trembling (Philippians 2:12-13). **Pray for His Guidance:** Ask Him to incline your heart to His ways (Psalm 119:35-36). **Praise Him for Good Works:** Acknowledge that even your willingness to do good comes from Him (1 Chronicles 29:14-19).[8]

3. How God Acts Without Sinning. God as the Supreme Mover: God acts as the first cause, while man is the subject in whom sin resides. The Sun shining on a dunghill produces a foul smell, but the Sun is not defiled. A clock with defective mechanisms strikes incorrectly when moved by a weight, but the fault lies with the clock, not the weight. A skilled musician playing an out-of-tune instrument creates discordant sounds, but the error lies in

---

[8] Much more to this purpose, see Augustine lib. 5. *contra Julian* c. 3.

the instrument. Similarly, man is the source of sin, while God, as the first mover, is *untainted*.

God as the Author of Nature: God acts according to His role as Creator, sustaining natural actions that are morally neutral in themselves. The moral quality of an act depends on man's obedience or disobedience to God's law. Adam's eating of the fruit was a natural act that became sinful only because it violated God's command. God's operation as Creator remains pure, even though Adam's action was morally corrupt.

God Acts According to a Pure Rule: God acts according to the perfect rule of His wisdom, which aims at His glory. Sinful actions, while fulfilling God's purposes, are performed by man in violation of God's law. The Jews crucifying Christ acted wickedly, yet they fulfilled *God's* predetermined counsel (Acts 2:23).

God's involvement in sinful actions is distinct from the sin itself. He moves as Creator and Governor, while man sins as a moral agent, acting contrary to God's law. Thus, God remains blameless, and man bears the guilt of his sin.

(Further objections and clarifications will follow in subsequent sections.)

The third basis upon which they argue that the doctrine of predestination makes God the author of sin is that God denied Adam the grace necessary to ensure, as to the event, his actual perseverance in righteousness.

To affirm that God is the author of sin is, by all accounts, blasphemy. Therefore, whatever Scripture teaches regarding God's actions toward man in the matter of Adam's first sin or fall cannot logically lead to the conclusion that God is the author of sin. The question then is: What does Scripture teach? We assert that Adam was indeed denied the grace necessary to ensure his perseverance, and this is evident from the following considerations.

First, Adam was created in the image of God (Genesis 1:26). This image included righteousness and true holiness (Ephesians 4:24). Adam's state was one of habitual righteousness, enabling him to will and perform all that was good according to the law of God written on his heart. His faculties were perfectly aligned to follow the rule of righteousness without interruption or deviation. Unlike the regenerate in their struggle, described in Romans 7:18 as willing good but lacking the ability to *fully* perform it, Adam had both the ability to will and to do *all* that was required of him. Furthermore, this righteousness and power to obey were not only his but also the inheritance of his posterity.

Second, Adam was denied the grace that would ensure his standing, as evidenced by his fall. God could have given him the effectual grace that would have prevented his fall, as He did for the angels who have kept their original state and will continue to do so forever. If such grace had been given to Adam, he would have stood firm, for it is contradictory to say that one has the grace to stand and yet does not stand. Adam possessed the power to will and do all good, but he was not given the grace to exercise that power. Just as a sound eye has the capacity to see but requires light to actualize sight, or as a finely tuned instrument requires the touch of a musician to produce harmonious sound, so too Adam's habitual righteousness required the actuating grace of God to ensure perseverance.

As Augustine observes, "The first man did not have that grace by which he could never do evil, but he had the grace by which he could avoid evil if he so willed. He had an aid of grace which he could forsake if he chose and in which he could remain if he willed, but not the grace by which he would will to remain."[9] Augustine further compares this to the grace given to believers in Christ, which is so great that not only do they have the ability to persevere if they will, but they are also given the will to persevere. "For in us," Augustine writes, "by the grace of God, there is both the ability to act and the will to act."

Third, Adam could not have received the grace that would ensure his standing because this would contradict God's plan and knowledge. Although Adam had habitual righteousness and the power to stand, he also required God's sustaining influence—an influx of light upon his mind and holiness upon his will—to actualize that power. This sustaining grace could not be given because Scripture is clear on two points:

1. God knew with certainty that Adam would fall. To deny God's eternal and infallible knowledge of Adam's fall—or of any event—is to undermine His omniscience, an

---

[9] Lib. *de correptione & grat.* c. 11.

essential attribute of His being. If God knew Adam would fall, it would be contradictory to suppose that He also gave Adam the grace to stand, for this would mean God knew with certainty that Adam would fall while also knowing with certainty that Adam might not fall.

2. God decreed Adam's fall. If God decreed that Adam would fall by His permission, then He could not have given Adam the grace that would ensure his perseverance without contradicting His own decree. To suppose otherwise would make God's administration of His creation capable of voiding His eternal purposes. To clarify, we affirm:

1. God decreed that all His works would serve His glory, which is the ultimate end of all things.
2. God decreed not only His glory in general but also the specific glory that would arise from each particular act and event.
3. God's decree comprehensively encompasses every aspect of His glory, including the glory arising from man's final state, which necessarily presupposes sin. Without sin, there would be no manifestation of God's mercy in salvation or His justice in condemnation. Thus, God decreed the fall of Adam and, through him, all humanity.

An objection is raised: why would God give Adam a righteous law, equip him with the habitual righteousness necessary to obey it, and yet decree that Adam would not fulfill it? The answer lies in *God's purpose to manifest His glory*.

Without a righteous law and Adam's subsequent violation of it, there would have been no sin, and thus no opportunity for the display of God's justice and mercy. Adam was created righteous, given a righteous law, and left to violate it by his own will. In this, Adam sinned, and we sinned in him.

Another objection is this: By what right does God condemn man for sinning when He decreed that man would sin and withheld the grace necessary to prevent it? The response is twofold.

First, whatever God wills is righteous simply *because* He wills it. His will is the ultimate standard of righteousness. When we ask, "Why has the Lord done this?" the only answer is, "Because it pleased Him." To demand a reason beyond His will is to seek something higher than God, which is impossible, as Augustine asserts.

Second, God asserts His dominion as Creator over man. Paul rebukes this very question, saying, "Nay but, O man, who art thou that repliest against God? Shall the thing formed say to him that formed it, Why hast thou made me thus?" (Romans 9:20). It is not for the creature to question the Creator, who has absolute authority over His creation. God, as the potter, has power over the clay to shape it as He pleases, whether for honorable or dishonorable use. Man, as a created being, has no standing to demand justification from the One who formed him.

The third objection claims that the doctrine of predestination makes God the author of sin because He denied Adam the grace necessary to ensure, as to the event, his perseverance in righteousness.

In answering this, we affirm that to accuse God of being the author of sin is blasphemy. Thus, whatever Scripture teaches about God's dealings with Adam concerning the first sin cannot lead to this conclusion. The question is: What does Scripture teach? We assert that Adam was denied the grace that would ensure his standing, and this can be demonstrated in the following ways.

First, Adam was created in the image of God (Genesis 1:26), which includes righteousness and true holiness (Ephesians 4:24). This state of habitual righteousness enabled him to will and perform all the good that God's law, written on his heart, required. His faculties were perfectly aligned to follow righteousness without deviation. Unlike the regenerate, described in Romans 7:18 as willing good but unable to fully perform it, Adam possessed both the ability to will and to act according to God's commands. This righteousness and ability to obey were inherent not only in Adam but also in his posterity.

Second, Adam's fall demonstrates that he was denied the grace necessary to ensure his perseverance. While God was able to give him such grace, as He gave the elect angels who have kept their first estate, He did not do so. If such grace had been granted, Adam would have stood firm, for it is contradictory to say that one possesses grace ensuring perseverance yet does not persevere. Adam had the power to will and to act according to righteousness, but the exercise of this power required further enabling grace, which was not granted. Just as a sound eye requires light to see, or a finely tuned instrument requires a musician to produce harmony, Adam's habitual righteousness required God's sustaining grace to ensure actual perseverance.

As Augustine writes, "The first man did not have that grace by which he could never do evil, but he had the grace by which he could avoid evil if he so willed. He had an aid of grace which he could forsake if he chose, and in which he could remain if he willed, but not the grace by which he would will to remain." Augustine also compares this grace to the greater aid given to believers in Christ, which ensures not only the ability to persevere but also the will to persevere. "In us, by the grace of God," he writes, "there is both the ability and the will to act."

Third, Adam could not have received the grace necessary to ensure his standing because it would have contradicted God's knowledge and decree. Although Adam had the power to stand, his standing as to the event depended on God's active grace. This grace could not be granted because:

1. God knew with certainty that Adam would fall. Denying God's infallible knowledge of Adam's fall—or any event—undermines His omniscience. If God knew Adam would fall, it would be contradictory to suppose He granted Adam the grace to ensure his standing. For if God knew Adam would fall, it could not simultaneously be true that Adam might not fall.

2. God decreed Adam's fall. God decreed that Adam would fall by His permission, and it was through this decree that He knew with certainty that Adam would fall. If Adam had received the grace to ensure his standing, it would have rendered God's decree void. God's decrees, however, cannot be frustrated.

To summarize this briefly, we affirm:

1. God decreed that all His works would serve His glory as their ultimate end.
2. God decreed not only His glory in general but also every specific manifestation of it.
3. God's decree includes all aspects of His glory, including the glory arising from man's fall and redemption. Without sin, there could be no display of God's justice in condemning sinners or His mercy in saving them. Thus, God decreed the fall of Adam as part of His purpose to glorify Himself.

An objection is raised: Why would God give Adam a righteous law, enable him with habitual righteousness to obey it, and yet decree that Adam would not fulfill it? The answer lies in God's purpose to manifest His glory. Without a righteous law and Adam's subsequent transgression, there could be no sin and, consequently, no display of God's justice and mercy. Adam sinned by violating a law he was commanded to keep and for which he had the ability to obey. In Adam's transgression, all humanity sinned.

Another objection claims it is unjust for God to condemn man for sinning when He decreed man's sin and withheld the grace necessary to prevent it. To this, we respond:

First, whatever God wills is righteous simply because He wills it. His will is the ultimate standard of righteousness. As Augustine writes, "When we ask, 'Why has the Lord done this?' the only answer is, 'Because it pleased Him.' To demand a reason beyond His will is to seek something higher than God, which cannot exist."[10]

Second, God asserts His absolute dominion as Creator over His creation. Paul rebukes such questioning: "Nay but, O man, who art thou that repliest against God? Shall the thing formed say to him that formed it, Why hast thou made me thus?" (Romans 9:20). The Creator has sovereign authority over His creation, just as a potter has power over the clay to shape it as he pleases.

Third, God's actions toward His creation are beyond human comprehension. His judgments are unsearchable, and His ways are past finding out (Romans 11:33). As Job was humbled before God's wisdom in creation, so must we acknowledge the limits of our understanding in God's decrees.

Thus, while Adam's fall and the sin of mankind manifest God's justice and mercy, the depths of His purposes remain beyond our grasp. We are called to trust in the wisdom and righteousness of God, whose ways are perfect even when they surpass our understanding.

---

[10] *De verbis Apostol.* Serm. 20.

The Sixth Sermon

The third objection argues that the doctrine of predestination undermines the liberty of man's will and, as a result, absolves him of all sin since liberty is deemed necessary for any sinful action. This objection rests on two points: first, that God has decreed man's sin; second, that God moves man's will, even when man wills sinfully, thereby determining it in its operation. From this, they conclude that man sins of necessity, not freely, and therefore his sin cannot truly be sin. The same objection is also raised concerning actions that are not sinful.

In response to the first point, the decree of God, we affirm: Scripture clearly teaches that the actions of man's will—both good and evil—are decreed by God. This has already been demonstrated, but we will provide specific examples. Concerning good actions: the conversion of a sinner is decreed (Romans 9:11; Romans 8:28-30; Acts 13:48); the faith and obedience of converted sinners are decreed (Ephesians 1:4; 2 Thessalonians 2:13); and the obedience of Christ in fulfilling the work of redemption was decreed (1 Peter 1:20; Hebrews 10:7). Concerning evil actions: the crucifixion of Christ by the Jews and Romans was decreed (Acts 4:27); Absalom's incest was decreed, as evidenced by God's prophecy (2 Samuel 12:11). Furthermore, all events foretold in Scripture as certain, not conditional (e.g., Nineveh's destruction, which was conditional), must have been decreed by God. Otherwise, God's word could be proven false. For instance, the bitter persecutions of the Church, the faith of the martyrs, the rage of mystical

Babylon, the faithfulness of the true Church, the conversion of the Jews, and the fullness of the Gentiles—all these are decreed and foretold. It is evident that the will and actions of men play a significant role in these decreed events.

1. The decree of God does *not* infringe upon the liberty of man's will because the decree itself is an act within God's own counsel. It does not change man's nature or condition until it is executed.
2. The decree actually establishes man's liberty. Because God has decreed that man shall will, it is certain that man shall will. God's counsels cannot fail. However, while it is certain that man shall will, it is equally certain that man shall will freely. To will inherently involves liberty. God decrees not only the existence of things and their actions but also their specific kinds and modes of operation. Just as He has ordained natural causes to work necessarily—such as fire burning—so He has ordained voluntary and contingent causes to work freely and contingently.

An objection arises: if God has decreed something, it must necessarily happen, or else His decree could be frustrated. To this, we respond:

It is true that what God decrees must necessarily happen, but this necessity is not one of compulsion or natural force. Instead, it is *a necessity of consequence*: the event must happen, but the manner of its occurrence depends on the nature of the cause. If the cause is free and contingent, the event will occur freely and contingently. Thus, there is necessity in the event but not in the cause. This necessity does not conflict with God's foreknowledge, nor does it impose compulsion on man's will.

Another objection questions whether the same effect can occur both necessarily and contingently. The answer is yes, provided we understand necessity correctly—not as absolute but as conditional. For example:

1. God created the world freely. It was in His power to create or not create, and to create this world or another. However, once He decreed creation, it became necessary for the world to exist, though the act of creation remained free.
2. When Christ was crucified, His legs were not broken to fulfill the prophecy that not a bone of Him would be broken. God's determination made it necessary for this prophecy to be fulfilled, yet the soldiers refrained from breaking His legs voluntarily.

In short, while God's decree establishes the certainty of events, it does not alter the manner of their occurrence. Events caused by free agents remain free, while those caused by necessary agents remain necessary.

The second point of the objection concerns God's motion upon the will of man, which they argue determines the will and thereby eliminates liberty. To address this, we must distinguish two types of liberty:

1. The liberty of independence, where the will acts without being moved by any higher cause, belongs solely to God. Only His will is entirely independent.

The wills of men and angels are subject to His dominion and are moved by Him. This has already been demonstrated, and many further arguments could be made, particularly concerning the doctrines of conversion and perseverance. However, these would be unnecessary digressions, as the point has been sufficiently established.

2. The liberty of choice, where the will acts according to its own inclinations and judgment, is the liberty possessed by men and angels. The will operates by choosing or refusing based on what it finds agreeable. In this liberty, the will acts with a sense of preference, either willing or refusing according to what it perceives as good or evil. While the will retains the power to choose otherwise, its actual choice aligns with the judgment of the understanding, which presents the object as desirable or undesirable.

This liberty of choice distinguishes man from necessary agents, such as fire, which acts without thought, or brute beasts, which act by instinct rather than reason. Man's will operates freely in response to the understanding's guidance.

To apply this to the objection: the liberty of independence, being peculiar to God, is not necessary for the creature. Where the liberty of choice exists, as described, the will remains free despite God's motion upon it.

The Sixth Sermon

Another objection asks how determination to one option can coexist with liberty of choice. There are two types of determination: 1. Determination to one of two moral objects (good or evil). This does not negate liberty. For example, God, Christ, angels, and glorified saints can only will good, yet their wills are perfectly free. Similarly, the devil, the damned, and the unregenerate can only will evil, yet their wills remain naturally free, though morally enslaved. Thus, determination to good or evil does not eliminate liberty.

2. Determination to one act (to *will* or to *nill*). This also does not destroy liberty. God moves the will by its own principles, using the understanding to direct it. By God's motion, the will acts freely, doing what it prefers in the light of the understanding while retaining the power to choose otherwise. Thus, the liberty of man's will remains intact, even under God's decree and motion. Any remaining objections are of lesser significance and are sufficiently addressed by the answers provided to these main objections.

FINIS

June 5, 1648.
Imprimatur
John Downame

Other Works Published by Puritan Publications that Deal with the Gangrene of Arminianism

Puritan Meditations by Francis Rous (1579–1659)
Whether you are seeking deeper communion with God or spiritual nourishment for life's challenges, "Puritan Meditations" provides a timeless roadmap toward the joy and peace found only in God's word and in Jesus Christ.

The Decision of Dordt: ONE TRUTH, Reformed Music Project by C. Matthew McMahon
It's amazing to be able to listen to good music, while at the same time having the depth of the Canons of the Synod of Dordt depicted without any compromise or shallowness.

The Efficiency of God's Grace in Bringing Gain-Saying Sinners to Christ by Simeon Ashe (d. 1662)
How does God draw sinners to himself? In this rare puritan work Simeon Ashe teaches on John 6:44, and the manner in which God uses to drag gain-saying sinners to salvation.

A Treatise of Man's Imagination by William Perkins (1558-1602)
William Perkins masterfully deals with total depravity in a practical framework. A helpful and convicting work on sin and the mind.

Other Works

A Brief Description of Heretics by Ephraim Pagitt (1575-1647)
Heresy in the church is exceedingly destructive. This work is a wonderful summation of many of the heresies that have plagued the church throughout history, as well as in our own day. Added to this work is also Obadiah Sedgwick's sermon on "The Nature and Danger of Heresies."

The All-Seeing Unseen Eye of God and Other Sermons by Matthew Newcomen (1610–1669)
This volume is a compilation of Newcomen's most rare sermons. "The All-Seeing Unseen Eye Of God" which is a fantastic exhortation to holiness demonstrates that God knows every person who ever was or will be, all their works, all their speeches, and all their thoughts, and such things are always present in the mind of God. This sermon alone is worth the cost of the volume. It is best exhortation on this subject matter in print.

Justification by Faith Alone by John Eedes (1609-1667)
If one were to be remembered in church history for one book written in a lifetime, what would it be? For John Eedes it is this work on Justification. Justification by faith alone is the cornerstone of the Gospel. It is not a physical act, but a judicial act; not by inherent righteousness, but God as Judge in the court of mercy by judicial declaration remits sin to the believer through Christ's merits, and absolves the sinner repenting, and believing. Eedes in this wonderful puritan work masterfully teaches this biblical doctrine, while at the

same time dismantles the unbiblical positions of the Dispensationalists, Antinomians, Arminians and the new justification doctrine taught by Richard Baxter.

Justification by Faith Alone by Jonathan Edwards (1703–1758)
In this classic work, Edwards covers the intricacies of how believers are made righteous only through Christ's merits, and that this justifying righteousness is equally imputed to all elect believers. This is accomplished by the condition of faith as an instrument. A classic work.

Presumptive Regeneration, or, the Baptismal Regeneration of Elect Infants by Cornelius Burgess (1589-1665)
Does anything actually happen when baptism is performed? This work by Burgess is a polemic which confirms the position of the Reformed Church throughout the centuries. It is a testament to believing the promises of God to his elect church, instead of merely discerning the intents of a profession before baptism by human standards. A must read!

The Substitutionary Atonement of Jesus Christ by Francis Turretin (1623-1687)
Anything written by the reformer Francis Turretin is usually AWESOME. This work is no exception and it focuses exclusively on Christ's atonement. Included in this second edition is a work on Turretin's covenant theology by C. Matthew McMahon.

Other Works

How Faith Works: Rescuing the Gospel from Contemporary Evangelicalism by C. Matthew McMahon.

What is the Biblical Gospel? Are you content to call yourself an "Evangelical?" Is the Evangelical Gospel the same Gospel of the Protestant Reformation? Is an Evangelical today the same as an evangelical during the time of Luther, Calvin or the Puritans? If the magisterial Reformers suddenly walked into your church today, would they be pleased with the Gospel that is being preached from its pulpit? This work covers the "gospel" of the contemporary church and the remedy found in the Gospel of Jesus Christ.

The Two Wills of God: Does God Really Have Two Wills? by C. Matthew McMahon

Does God have two wills? It sure does seem like He does when on the one hand, "our God is in the heavens He doth whatsoever He pleases," and then "God repenteth that He made man..." What do we make of this and other seemingly difficult passages in the bible about God's will? This work will lay to rest the tension between orthodox Calvinism, and deviant Arminianism.

www.ingramcontent.com/pod-product-compliance
Lightning Source LLC
Chambersburg PA
CBHW020857160426
43192CB00007B/966